HEALING WITH TREES:

Finding a Path to Wholeness

Margaret Cheasebro, Ph.D.

Margaret Cheasebro
8-25-2024

Author Photo by Tony Bennett.
Cover design by vibrant_grafiz of fiverr.com

Library of Congress Cataloging-in-Publication Data

Names: Cheasebro, Margaret, 1945- author.
Title: Healing with trees : finding a path to wholeness / Margaret Cheasebro, Ph.D.
Description: Albuquerque : Casa de Snapdragon LLC, 2017.
Identifiers: LCCN 2017004639 | ISBN 9781937240790 (pbk.)
Subjects: LCSH: Trees--Miscellanea. | Healing--Religious aspects. | Spirituality.
Classification: LCC BF1623.P5 C44 2017 | DDC 133/.258216--dc23
LC record available at https://lccn.loc.gov/2017004639

20170315
Casa de Snapdragon LLC
12901 Bryce Avenue, NE
Albuquerque, NM 87112
casadesnapdragon.com

Printed in the United States of America

We are equal partners with all that exists, co-creators with trees and galaxies and the microorganisms in our own gut, in a materially and spiritually evolving universe.

– Richard Schiffman

Evidence now supports the vision of the poet and the philosopher that plants are living, breathing, communicating creatures, endowed with personality and the attributes of soul.

– Peter Tompkins and Christopher Bird in *The Secret Life of Plants*

It is fact: man can and does communicate with plant life. Plants are living objects, sensitive, rooted in space. They may be blind, deaf and dumb in the human sense, but there is no doubt in my mind that they are extremely sensitive instruments for measuring man's emotions. They radiate energy forces that are beneficial to man. One can feel these forces! They feed into one's own force field, which in turn feeds back energy to the plant.

– Research chemist Marcel Vogel

All life forms – trees, plants, dogs, cats, everything – have the same geometric and structural patterns running through them that ran through you when you were microscopic.

– Drunvalo Melchizedek

To my late husband, Wally. Though he did not always understand my connection with trees, he always supported my relationship with them.

HEALING WITH TREES:

FINDING A PATH TO WHOLENESS

Part I: Meeting the Trees
Part II: A Wealth of Tools

Margaret Cheasebro, Ph.D

Contents

PART I

MEETING THE TREES

INTRODUCTION

DISCOVERING THE TREES

As I child, I loved to climb trees. As an adult, I enjoy having trees in my yard. They provide shade and beauty. They shelter animals and promote a healthy environment. But never in my wildest dreams did I think I could communicate with trees. That changed when a Reiki Master suggested I write a book about our connection with trees. I'd never thought about being connected with trees, and I wasn't sure what would come of exploring such a tie.

I have always seen myself as dependable, hardworking, well organized, a perfectionist at times, seldom on the fringes. My most unorthodox activity, up to that point, had been studying to become a Reiki Master. Reiki is a form of energy that promotes relaxation and balance so the body can do a better job of healing itself. Interacting with the trees stretched me and opened my understanding in new ways, beyond what I had learned in my study and practice of Reiki.

I began to spend more time with trees, focusing on the ones in my yard. Quickly, I realized they each had distinct personalities. An Austrian pine seemed austere. A maple complained and worried. A cottonwood sent love. When I traveled, I spent time communicating with trees wherever I went. When I saw a tree near the side of the road, my patient husband would pull over so I could spend a little time with it.

I learned more about communicating with trees when a man and a woman came into my life in the fall of 2008. They had a relationship with the Earth unlike anything I had known. I learned more about that connection as we walked among the trees on and near my property. Conversing with trees and other elements in nature were as natural to the woman as breathing. She talked with trees as though they were old friends. She could pick up a stone and hear its story. She understood what the river had to say. The man sensed the fears and strengths of trees. He could send the energy of water to where it was needed. We had deep conversations as we walked among the trees. Some grew by an irrigation ditch across the road from our house. Others flourished beside the nearby Animas River. At first, trees weren't sure they could trust us. Their experience with humans has not always been positive. The more time we spent with them, the more their trust level grew. Though there is nothing unusual about my property, it began to feel like holy ground as we forged a relationship with the trees laced with prayer and mutual respect.

When my friends moved on, I continued my relationship with nature. The trees became my teachers and friends. I checked on them each visit to see if they were all right, if they needed anything from me, and if they had something to tell me. I prayed for them and sent them Reiki. If a tree was not doing well, it responded instantly to prayer and Reiki.

Junipers, cottonwoods, Russian olives and elms are the most common species of trees on and near our property, though there are some fruit trees, maples and towering pines. I visited all of them that wanted to interact with me. They each have their own personalities and their own way of communicating. Cottonwoods are nurturing and loving. They taught me about staying grounded and balancing the masculine and feminine energies within me. Junipers have deep connections with the non-physical realm. Elms are often reserved and can be great healers. Russian olives are protective and loyal. One apricot tree shared its angelic connection and the work its angels do to spread peace and harmony to all life that inhabits our planet.

Through my growing relationship with trees, I understood that when I connected with them, I was really connecting with my own inner being, the vast part of me that lies beyond my physical body. When I interact with trees, I am intuitively reminded of the power, wisdom and divine nature that lies at my core and at the core of every tree. That's not surprising, because trees are part of God's creation. We all have that connection with Oneness, though it's easy to forget who we really are when we face challenges and struggles.

When I write that a tree said something to me, what I mean is that as I focus on a tree I am able to hear the wisdom of my connection to the One that unites us all. I am able to better hear my own Higher Self, that spiritual part of me that is much vaster and wiser than my physical self. It has a deep connection with the One, with God, Source, All that Is, or whatever you prefer to call divinity. As I merge my attention with the trees, my consciousness rises to a higher level, which helps me to better hear the trees and their loving, nurturing, encouraging messages.

When I visited my son in Alaska, a birch tree there caught my attention. It had a message for both me and the trees back home: "Open your heart." When we open our hearts, we can more easily communicate with nature and sense the Oneness that we all share. It is through our hearts, through unconditional love, that we most effectively connect with trees.

For a long time, my relationship with trees was a private experience. I was afraid if I told anyone else, they'd think I was crazy or weird. As I cautiously related some experiences, I was relieved to find people interested and sometimes intrigued. When I shared my experiences with my best friend, who has walked with me on healing and spiritual pathways for many years, she too could sense a connection with the trees. Whenever I learned a new healing exercise from the trees, I shared it with her, and she practiced each one. She reported her experiences to me, which reinforced my trust in what the trees were telling me.

I later met a healer with strong connections to angels who also has a deep connection with trees. She understands them and recognizes their need to be acknowledged and appreciated. She affirmed what I have come to know, that it really is possible to communicate with trees and that they want to link with people they can trust.

To optimize my own health, I sometimes go to a naturopath who practices several forms of alternative healing techniques. He can see through the veil separating the physical from non-physical in ways I can't – yet. Several trees who know me sometimes come to the healing sessions and tell him how to work with me. "I'm not familiar with this technique," he often says, but he tried them all, and they work in ways that sometimes amaze him.

As time passed, during those sessions the trees began to move healing energy through my body without his help, realigning and improving pathways so that my energy stayed at a higher level. I could feel the movement, and the practitioner could see it. "I've never seen anything like this before!" he would exclaim. That has become a common refrain during our sessions as the trees continue to demonstrate their healing abilities. Trees often assist him as he works with other clients, and they have been present when I work with my own clients as well.

Many trees want to communicate with us and to help us reconnect with the majesty of who we really are. They have messages to share, healing to offer, and understandings about the nature of our Earth to reveal. They offer to help us, and they ask us to help them. When we spend time among trees, we can find a pathway to our own inner wisdom, to greater health, and to the Oneness that connects us all.

CHAPTER 1

DEEPENING THE RELATIONSHIP

As my relationship deepened with the trees, it seemed important to share with more people what they've taught me. Because I wasn't sure how to tell such an unusual story or how it would be received, for more than a year I just kept visiting the trees and feeling amazed by what they taught me.

Then one day, the Healing Tree, an ancient, scarred cottonwood by the irrigation ditch bridge, stopped communicating with me. "There's no point in telling you more," it said, "until you share what you've already learned." I gulped. If I related those things, people might brand me as bizarre or worse. Several days later, the Power Tree, a magnificent cottonwood, conveyed deep sadness, a sense of things left undone.

Not long after that, I drove to the country home of a certified clinical herbologist to interview her for an article I was writing for a local publication. She wasn't there. She'd forgotten about the interview, her husband said, but she would return from town in a couple of hours. While I waited, he showed me the gardens behind their house. As we approached a small ash tree at the far end of an herb patch, I felt a deep ache coming from it. It needed help. Stopping, I asked the man, "What do you know about this tree?"

"I gave it to my wife as an anniversary present," he replied. "On a metaphysical level, it's the male counterpart of the female hawthorn growing over there." He pointed to a tree near the back of their home. As we walked through the gardens toward the house, he explained that his wife had undergone a hysterectomy the year before. In a ceremony, she and some friends buried the surgical remains under the hawthorn and marked the spot with a handmade plaque. The beautiful tree near the house showed no outward signs of turmoil, but as I approached it, the hawthorn's grief overwhelmed me. As I wept, I prayed that God would provide the tree with whatever it needed to heal. As the hawthorn's grief dissipated, my emotions calmed too. I looked at the heart shaped stone under the tree that marked the burial spot. Peace settled over both of us.

When the herbologist came home, she took me on a more extended tour of the gardens. I passed the ash tree again. This time, it felt calm, and I understood what had happened. During the burial ceremony, the human emotions of grief had overwhelmed the hawthorn. The ash did its best to shoulder its partner's sadness, but the burden was too great. By acknowledging the trees and their needs, I lent them strength. Prayer helped the hawthorn return to wholeness.

A few days later when I visited the Power Tree, waves of love and joy flowed from it. The sense of things undone had vanished. By befriending the ash and hawthorn and praying for their needs, I had somehow created a bond of trust between the trees and me. They knew they could trust me to help them. And they, in turn, offered to help me. Since then, wherever I go I feel love coming from trees I've never met. They want to be acknowledged and respected for what they have to offer. They love to receive Reiki, and they soak up prayer like a sponge. Because their response to prayer is instantaneous, I realize more than ever what a powerful tool prayer is for all of us.

Trees that want to communicate have revealed their names to me. On a few occasions, they've changed their names to relate deeper aspects of what they have to offer, but they assure me that either name is okay. The names, it seems, are for my convenience.

CHAPTER 2

THE HEALING TREE

I am strong, solidly grounded, a lookout, guardian and healer.

This aging cottonwood stands near the irrigation ditch bridge. Some of its branches are dead. As it grew weaker with the passing years, it faced its decline with a defiant refusal to give up. It carried the same fear that most trees carry - a dread of being cut down so they can no longer play their vital role of keeping the planet healthy. They absorb carbon dioxide exhaled by people and animals and produce oxygen that we need for survival. They offer shelter, food, and erosion control.

The more that friends and I acknowledged the Healing Tree and communicated with it, the more trusting the cottonwood became. It regained strength. I came to know it as a leader, guardian and healer. It often connects over long distances with people to whom it feels a bond, and it helps us to stay grounded.

Not long after I began communicating with the tree, I saw a black ball of energy inside the base of its trunk just below ground level. The tree seemed stressed. The energy was stuck in the black ball, keeping the tree from using it to heal itself. As I visualized tunnels through its roots and up into its trunk, the freed energy followed those tunnels, and the tree began to heal.

A week later, I noticed the cottonwood had trouble grounding on its south side. In the space that the black ball of energy once occupied stood what resembled a tombstone. Long before we bought this property, a family with two boys had lived in our house and climbed the Healing Tree, using wooden steps they'd nailed to its trunk. The boys loved to swim in the irrigation ditch, and one of them drowned there. The cottonwood still grieved for the boy and wished it could have saved him. My two friends with gifted nature connections suggested that I ask the boy's spirit to visit the tree. When I made that request, the boy immediately appeared, standing by its trunk, and intense joy burst from the tree. When I asked the boy to stay with the cottonwood, he climbed it, and his spirit has stayed there ever since.

When my best friend came to visit, her lungs drenched with toxins from second hand cigarette smoke, she felt the tree's spirit touch her lungs and reduce her congestion. I watched smoke waft from her back and float away.

Though the Healing Tree has always responded to that name, it prefers the name Grandfather. It is a grandfather tree, full of wisdom and compassion. It knows what goes on around it, and it provides loving leadership. When I call it Grandfather, it energetically stands taller. There is a sense of power, steadfastness and courage about the Grandfather Tree, and the name suits its personality.

Sometimes it sends energy to me through its roots. That energy travels from my feet through my body, out the top of my head and up to the top of the tree. Then it loops down through the tree to complete a circle between us. In this way we not only share our knowledge but we help to balance and strengthen each other's energy.

If you would like to try this with a tree, stand beside it and let it know how much you enjoy and appreciate it. If you feel so inclined, touch its bark with your hands. When you feel a connection with it, imagine energy flowing between you and the tree. You may feel the energy start at your feet or at another part of your body. Or you may feel it start from the tree and then move to you. Allow the energy to move through you and the tree in whatever pattern it chooses to take. Enjoy the moment and the strength it gives to both of you.

Once when I stood by the cottonwood and wondered if I should risk sharing what the trees have taught me, it counseled, "Be bold!" Slowly, carefully, I began to share my experiences with the trees. Eventually I became bolder and even led a workshop about how to connect with trees.

After someone taught me a grounding exercise involving connecting my solar plexus chakra to the Earth's core, the Healing Tree let me know there was more to that exercise. It showed me how to grow roots from my feet and to let those roots flow into the center of the Earth. From there, energy flowed through those roots up into my body, filling not just my solar plexus but every aspect of myself. Once the energy filled me, I was to retract the roots from the Earth's center back into my feet and feel the power of my connection with this planet.

Of all the cottonwood's gifts to me, perhaps the greatest one came more than two years after I began to communicate with it. On a late October day, it worked hard to create what looked like a wide, brownish red path that traveled from its roots just below its trunk into my feet and up through my body. As that brownish red path reached my heart, I felt a surge of power. When the path moved from my heart toward my throat, it blossomed into white, blue, green, purple and orange colors. Energy burst into my throat, flowed out the top of my head, and looped back through my head down to my heart, where it branched into my arms and hands. I felt my attitudes soften, my feelings grow more tender, and my cells buzz with vitality. The cottonwood had just transferred the essence of all its knowledge to me.

Over the following weeks, as energy flowed better through me, other trees benefited also. When I practiced exercises they had taught me to let our energies mingle, their own energy became healthier too. Even though the cottonwood continues to face challenges of growing older, a stronger energy courses through it. There is no doubt that we benefit each other.

From the naturopathic healer who can see the trees' spirits, I learned a playful exercise that all trees, including the Healing Tree, love. Between my hands, I form a plasma ball of energy, letting it grow and grow. I compress it together as my hands move closer together, then let it expand into a bigger ball as I move my hands farther apart. When the plasma ball is big enough, I throw it to a tree. It's such a delightful exercise that it makes me laugh to do it, and the trees seem to laugh as well.

My best friend, who has shared many experiences among the trees with me, called one day. She said that after a hard week on the job, made worse by the stresses of an irregular work schedule, the Healing Tree came to her in spirit. Long distance, it sent energy from its roots, through the ground, up through her feet and into her body, forming a loop between it and her. Through that loop, it washed away the negative energy and thoughts that had built up in her, cleared them out, and returned them to her as clean, positive energy. She felt revitalized.

In October 2012, I met a woman I recognized as my next teacher. In a series of workshops, she taught me a shamanic pathway. Before the first workshop, she instructed me to find three rocks that would represent aspects of the south direction. That direction involves helping to shed our false beliefs and thought patterns that no longer serve us well and to live in beauty with no judgment, no suffering and no attachment to the outcome. As I went to look for those stones, the Healing Tree let me know how important this training would be for me. It pointed out one of the south stones, which lay near the base of its trunk. During the training, I recognized that the trees are part of my lineage of helpers.

While visiting Spokane, Washington a year later, I felt drawn to a beautiful Ponderosa pine named Jonathan, who expressed great joy at being acknowledged and appreciated. After I had completed my shamanic training, the Healing Tree and Jonathan worked with me during a session to re-pattern and improve energy pathways through my body. Since then, both of them sometimes come to help when I do healing sessions for others.

The first time I realized they were both working through me to help someone else, my best friend had phoned to talk about health issues she faced. I could feel the energy of Jonathan and the Healing Tree move through my body as they showed me where they were helping her.

She sensed energy flowing through her body as well, and she began to heal physically and emotionally. For most of her life she had felt unworthy to receive love. The trees helped me understand that my friend's cells had stopped absorbing most nourishment from food because she believed her cells were not worthy to receive the food's life giving energy. Rail thin, she'd been losing weight and struggling with low energy.

As the trees sent positive energy flowing through her body, she began to heal. For the first time, she understood that she really was worthy to receive love. That message reached her cells, which now accept life giving energy from the food she eats. She called me 10 days later with the exciting news that she had gained 10 pounds and felt stronger and healthier than she had in years. I've often been aware of the powerful assistance of trees. It adds a deeper dimension to my healing work.

An irrigation ditch rider, who took care of the ditch and controlled the amount of water flowing through it, worried that, because the Healing Tree is getting old and brittle, some of its branches might fall into the ditch and clog the water flow. He told me the ditch company wanted to cut it down. Briefly, I explained how important this cottonwood is. When the man left, I tried to prepare the tree for all possible outcomes. In the end, the ditch rider only cut off some large branches that overhung the ditch. The Healing Tree didn't like losing big limbs, but it endured by grounding deeply into the Earth while it was being cut. It survived, and its non-physical vitality remains strong.

Though the years have taken their toll, the Healing Tree is not ready to call it quits. Once it let me know, "Don't give up on things that seem to be dead. They can flourish again."

CHAPTER 3

PORTAL TREE

I am a great communicator, and I connect all of us together.

A juniper, the Portal Tree is a master at making connections and communicating universal truths. Often when I visit this tree, I feel that I'm standing on holy ground.

It contains the knowledge of the history of all that has transpired between trees and people. Though it had forgotten some of that history, it has started to remember it and to share it with humans. The memories tell of a time when people and trees honored each other as valued beings, each with their own personalities, strengths and skills. Then, as people forgot that understanding, they began to misuse and devalue trees. As a result, trees distrusted people and stopped communicating with them, ending an alliance that once helped both to thrive. Now we are reawakening to the memory of how good and satisfying that relationship once was, and we are starting to remember how to communicate with each other in mutual respect once again.

Among other nuggets of wisdom the Portal Tree remembers is that the joy of doing what we love helps to manifest what we want. That joy naturally draws good things to us.

The juniper has a deep connection with the Oneness that connects us all. It can be a portal to other dimensions. One day the tree let me know I would soon travel through it to many dimensions beyond Earth and the stars. The juniper would benefit by recharging itself with the energy and wisdom I encountered. I imagined forging pathways through the tree, but on the day the adventure dawned, I didn't travel through the juniper. Instead, in my mind I saw a bright rectangular light in the shape of a door and simultaneously felt the base of my brain enlarge into endless switchbacks. Without ever leaving my brain, I began expanding outward, traveling to what looked like many stars except that it all happened within me. I contain the entire universe and beyond within myself! Like a hologram, I am just a piece of it all, and yet I am all of it. That day, the Portal Tree taught me that the universe is in me. Everything lies within me, from the farthest point in the vast universe to the smallest cell in my body. I go inward to everywhere. It is the way I experience the ever expanding love of God's nature. It is abundance in a way I had never understood it.

The Portal Tree once showed me an exercise to clear negative energy. I saw a huge counterclockwise semi-circle traveling from my left foot up to my head. At my head, it stopped moving counterclockwise and plunged straight down from my head to my feet. At my feet, it formed a clockwise semi-circle that moved from my right foot back up to my head. At my head, it formed a line that once again plunged down to my feet, where it formed a counterclockwise semi-circle that ascended from my left foot back up to my head, repeating the motions until all negative energy, including past programming that no longer serves me well, was replaced with positive energy.

As I communicate with the Portal Tree, I feel connected to the vastness of the Universe. At the same time, I am grounded to the Earth and sense my connection to power, to great love, and to fearlessness. As I carry that strength and love within me, I recognize that others whom I encounter can experience it too. When I grasp that concept, the Portal Tree echoes in my mind, "Yes! That's what it's all about!"

CHAPTER 4

CELEBRATING TREE

I have compassion for the physical ailments of others.

A juniper, the Celebrating Tree stretches tall branches upward toward the busy county road above the irrigation ditch. It celebrated the joy of life until years ago one of its branches snapped, barely connecting it with the rest of the tree. It felt traumatized. Barely clinging to life, the branch droops on the ground.

When trees want to connect with me, they draw my attention in a way that's hard to miss. This tree had never made itself known to me. I learned its name after my best friend, who has suffered many health challenges, came to visit. The tree introduced itself to her, letting her know that after facing the loss of its limb, it forgot how to enjoy life. When my friend focused on the tree, prayed for it and sent it Reiki, a surge of joy rushed through the juniper as it remembered how to celebrate life. Excitement buzzed through nearby trees as they witnessed the change in the juniper. My friend's own sense of wellbeing increased as she shared the joy of all the trees who watched the juniper's transformation. She called it the Celebrating Tree, because it not only remembered how to celebrate life, but it remembered how to celebrate it in a deeper, more grateful way than before it was wounded.

Anytime I have a physical ailment, the Celebrating Tree expresses great compassion and a desire to help. It comforts others who have physical ailments as well. It looks beyond their weaknesses, focuses on their strengths, and encourages them to move forward. It reminds us all to focus on the joy of living.

On one visit it reminded me to look beyond people's weaknesses and notice their strengths. When I focus on others' strengths, it helps their own strengths to develop. It was an important reminder, because when I get stressed it's easier to notice the negatives than the positives. I would much rather reinforce strengths than weaknesses, both in myself and others.

Sometimes the tree lets me know that it wants recognition and acknowledgement for the way it has moved forward in spite of tragedy. What a great reminder that we all need occasional recognition for our achievements.

I wasn't aware of feeling depleted when I visited the Celebrating Tree one day. After greeting it, praying for it and sending it Reiki, I walked on to the next tree, but I felt sadness floating from the juniper. I returned to it and tried to connect with what it had to tell me. "I'm not done," it seemed to say. "I want to help you." I didn't think I needed help, but as the tree worked with me, I felt a wealth of energy and love filling my solar plexus. Somehow I'd failed to notice how depleted I'd felt. I left my visit with the Celebrating Tree charged up and ready to handle anything.

CHAPTER 5

FRESH START TREE

I let go of past mistakes and make a fresh start.

This juniper, though small in size, recognizes the value of not dwelling on past mistakes. Those errors, it reminds me, are sometimes blessings in disguise. They can lead to unforeseen opportunities. Moving forward into new possibilities is better than wallowing in guilt and shame over past blunders.

The first time I noticed this tree, it felt very negative. Something didn't seem right. I called on Archangel Michael and other archangels, asking them to remove whatever negative influence was in the tree. Energetically, the juniper shook itself off and felt healthy again. I could feel its relief and gratitude. It had let a negative influence overtake it because the juniper felt too weak and unsure of itself to push it away. Since then, it has become powerful and now has the strength to refuse anything that doesn't feel right to it. It has grown so much because it's learned to forgive itself for past mistakes.

The summer that my son graduated from college and moved away, I felt sad. I missed him so much. While I stood in front of the Fresh Start Tree, I felt a line of love forming between the juniper and me, almost like a conveyor belt. I felt so filled with the healing salve of love that the ache of missing my son wasn't quite so hard to bear. The Fresh Start Tree has not only become a stronger, more confident tree; it has learned how to heal others as well.

CHAPTER 6

DISCERNMENT TREE

I know my limitations. I decline to do what I cannot handle and what is unhealthy for me.

Deeply grounded in the Earth and connected to the sky, the Discernment Tree draws strength from those attachments. It knows when not to take on tasks that will overwhelm it or that require more skills than it has.

I learned from this juniper that the awareness of our limitations is a sign of strength. It taught me the importance of saying no to tasks for which I don't have the time, desire, energy, or skills to do well.

This tree often stays in the background, not communicating much, but when it chooses to engage, the message is powerful. I experienced that power when it told me a memory of a past life would soon come up to help me understand why change sometimes seems fearful to me. When the memory emerged, I discovered I had been part of a poor peasant family in central France in the late 1700s. They had so many children they couldn't take care of us all, so when I was 14 they sold me to a farm family. Life was hard, and the work never seemed to end, though there were a few restful moments. When I was 17, the farm family sold me to another family, and life took on a never ending cycle of work and constant fatigue. I was malnourished and felt alone and unvalued. A few years later I died in my sleep, totally spent. Each change in that life had led to something worse. As a result, in my current life change sometimes made me feel apprehensive. Once the memory of that life returned, change no longer made me feel afraid. Was that memory really from a past life? I don't know, but once I "remembered" it, the fear left.

Sometimes when I walk past the Discernment Tree, it calls me back. As I stand near it, I feel so much love flowing from it to me. This quiet, unassuming tree knows its strengths and abilities and recognizes its limitations. Honoring itself gives it the strength to respect and love others, including me.

CHAPTER 7

ELEPHANT TREE

I am abundance. Trust that there is enough for all.

The Elephant Tree, a cottonwood, offers the assurance that we can work together to create a positive, healthy, abundant atmosphere. An encourager, it carries the essence of wholeness, connection and the total absence of judgment. It opens my understanding to possibilities, and it exudes love and lighthearted happiness. When I stand near this tree, I feel the vastness and presence of All that Is, of the Oneness that connects us all.

Once when I hired someone to clear a piece of our land and prepare it for planting, the Elephant Tree, which stands not far from that land, felt frightened by the heavy machinery. As many trees do, it feared that it would be cut down. I prayed for it, asked the angels to surround it and protect it, and assured it that it would be safe. It relaxed right away.

At other times I have done the Streams of Light Energy exercise with this cottonwood to reinforce the memory of its connection with God and the Earth. Afterwards, it becomes more calm and alert. The Streams of Light Energy exercise, which can be found in the exercise section at the end of Part 1, is a way of connecting to the divine presence and to the Earth in a healthy, nurturing way. You can read more about it in this section under "The Teaching Tree."

One day when I was unhappy with the progress of a project, the cottonwood reminded me that I could express thanks for the wonderful job being done and for the amazing skills that people brought to the project. The tree counseled that such an attitude would help to bring about improvement, and it did.

CHAPTER 8

EAGLE TREE

I am grounded in ancient truths.

This cottonwood sees from a higher perspective. At times, it seems to be all business and no nonsense, very structured in its purpose.

The enormity of the universe fills this tree, and sometimes it buzzes with the energy of ancient knowledge. It sees the big picture. It helps me to remember I am connected with all the wisdom I have ever encountered. It helps me speak what I know to be true with authority and confidence. As many other trees have done, it lets me know that it contains the entire universe within it, including me.

Long ago when a different family owned the property on which the Eagle Tree grows, some children threw a wire attached to a tire swing over one its large branches. With time, the branch died and fell. I felt sad for the tree's loss, but it assured me that by losing that branch it let go of a past that no longer served it well.

When I sense how deeply the Eagle Tree anchors into the ground, creating a bond much deeper than its physical roots, it reminds me that I too have a bond with the Earth. Remembering that bond will help me recall all the Earth wisdom I have ever known so that I can speak that knowledge with authority and confidence.

CHAPTER 9

JANE TREE

I live gracefully even in the face of adversity.

Jane's tall, thin trunk supports two large branches, one of which is dead. The other thrives. It faces the challenge of a dead limb with determination and a lightness of heart.

This cottonwood often reminds me that we are all connected, interwoven, part of the whole. It likes to do the Father Sky, Mother Earth exercise, a grounding technique, with me that can be found in the Exercises section at the end of Part I. In that exercise, I follow its roots deep into the Earth and feel myself flow even deeper. Then I soar up through its trunk and branches, embracing the sky. Down and up in a continuous loop the tree and I fly, strengthening our connection with Earth and sky. It shows me that when we stay grounded, we can let go of useless, emotional baggage.

One day when I felt lonely, Jane reminded me that we are all connected. I am never alone. The tree showed me how grounded it can be when it stays firmly focused on its purpose.

It likes to be recognized and acknowledged for the challenges it has faced and for the ability to keep an unswerving eye on its goal. In spite of its determination, it sometimes needs help. That's when I pray for it and thank it for its perseverance. It immediately perks up. It just needs to be affirmed.

CHAPTER 10

TWINKLING LIGHTS TREE OR POWER TREE

I have great power, love and compassion. I long to help others find joy.

Like bobbing, twinkling lights, this tree loves to shower encouragement, comfort and love on others. It often carries a feminine emphasis, and that's when I call it the Twinkling Lights Tree. It loves to nurture others and lend them strength. When I sense its powerful masculine essence, I refer to it as the Power Tree.

This cottonwood carries great love. When I'm near it, I feel my own heart expand. It urges me to stay grounded in love, because that's where the power is. It has a deep connection with its Creator.

As all trees do, this tree has a deeper, stronger, ancient aspect of itself that is so powerful it seems to flow with a golden energy like molten lava. When this deeper aspect revealed itself to me, it did so with a great longing to be recognized and to connect with me. When I allowed that connection to occur, I felt a geyser of joy engulf me. I asked what its name was, and it let me know the sounds are so different from what are familiar to me that I would not be able to pronounce the name, but Alayla comes close.

Though the tree is a complete whole, the two aspects of itself that have been with it from the time it was a seedling. Those two parts are its physical trunk, roots, branches, and leaves as well as Alayla, its powerful non-physical self.

Just as we have both a conscious and an unconscious mind that help to make up who we are, the two parts of a tree have a similar makeup. Though the two parts of each tree cannot precisely be compared to our conscious and unconscious mind, the analogy is helpful. The physical purpose of trees is somewhat similar to our conscious mind, which is aware of its contribution to the physical wellbeing of the Earth. In that aspect of themselves, trees provide shade, erosion control, shelter for animals, and beauty. The non-physical part of a tree could be roughly equated to our unconscious mind, which contains a vast amount of information that we don't even realize we have but that controls most of our actions and opinions. In the tree, that non-physical energy connects with the vast knowledge of the universe, and this is what drives its molten core of power. I find it healing and invigorating to be around both aspects of the Power Tree's energy.

At times, the physical tree surrounds me in protection and love. It forms a shield around me that keeps me from giving my energy away when I face challenging or confusing situations. Whenever I find my energy draining from me, the tree stops the outward flow and directs it back to me so that I feel reinvigorated. When I am surrounded by the Power Tree, I feel wrapped in love, and I know I'm not alone. At the same time, its non-physical, enormously powerful core, Alayla, connects me with a rich flow of knowledge coming from the universe.

It is one of several trees that teach me how to balance the masculine and feminine energy of doing and being in my body. A simple technique is to imagine an old fashioned scale with a tray on each side. On one tray put your masculine energy. On the other tray place your feminine energy. Then watch the scale until the two trays balance.

In spite of its powerful nature, when I first recognized I had a connection with the Power Tree, it expressed fear of being cut down. I sent Reiki to it, and a friend who sensed its power spoke assuring words to it. Its confidence grew as it recognized the protection we wrapped it in.

One night a few weeks after I realized this tree and I could communicate, I woke up feeling that in spirit I was in the uppermost branches of the Twinkling Lights Tree, which cradled me. I felt safe, loved and peaceful there, but I don't remember how my spirit got there. I have a strong bond with this cottonwood. When it is near me, either in its physical or non-physical form, I feel strongly grounded.

A few weeks after that incident in the tree's branches, the cottonwood let me know it had a powerful gift for me, something it had never given to anyone else. It wasn't sure I was strong enough to receive it or if I would use it wisely. Over the next three years it continued to feed me pieces of this gift until I had collected eleven different categories of tools with ten tools in each category for a total of 110 amazing tools. They provide help with everything from healing, protection and communication to business, marketing and leadership. They are included in the second part of this book so that anyone may use them. The gifts came with a sort of roadmap, which looked like an uneven oval, superimposed on the trunk of the tree. That oval contained blue circles that marked destinations and red lines that connected those circles like a highway. The blue circles twinkled and reminded me of stars. Every blue circle on the map marks a place or state of mind that contains information about one of the sets of ten tools. Over the coming months, true to its word, the tree brought me to those places and taught me how to use the tools.

On another night I woke up, thinking about the tree and imagining myself standing in front of it, wanting to give it a hug. It's such a huge tree that my arms would barely stretch one fifth of the way around it. Even so, I hugged as much of it as I could. Because it seems like such a powerful tree, I asked it to show me its core. Immediately, from inside the trunk poured smoke and heat like the awesome power of an erupting volcano. Water gushed from deep in the ground and up through the tree's trunk. I was viewing a primordial creation scene of incredible strength. It was the spirit of Alayla before I knew Alayla's name. The spirits of bear and eagle have deep connections to this tree.

No matter what challenges the Power Tree faces, it feels confident of the outcome. When I asked how it could know the outcome, it replied, "Because I Am." This tree knows that it is part of God's creation, connected to God and one with God in the same way that we are One. It remembers how powerful it is. On another day, it told me, "Be still and know that I Am." It urged me to be still and remember that I too am One with All that Is. I too am powerful.

This tree and I can travel anywhere together. There are no barriers. We make each other strong, and we help each other accomplish things we could not do alone.

Soon, this cottonwood began showing up at Reiki and cranio-sacral therapy sessions that were provided by the naturopathic healer who can see through the veil. When the Power Tree first showed up, the healer described him as a huge cottonwood with a strong male presence and a deep base voice, about five octaves deeper than a base drum. During one session, the tree asked the naturopath to have me stand near the tree when I went home. The tree needed me standing close by so it could pick up information that trees in Alaska had given to me when I visited my son there. I had no idea that any trees in Alaska had given me a message, but when I got home in the early evening, I stood near the Power Tree and let the message of the Alaska trees flow to the cottonwood. As the Power Tree connected with the message, I too understood it: Have hope. Be fearless. Enjoy life.

The Power Tree, the Healing Tree, and a few other trees routinely make an appearance at almost every session I have with the naturopath. They remind him to remove his rubber soled shoes before he works on me so he can stay better grounded. They give him instructions on how to handle challenging parts of my treatment, and he follows their directions even though the techniques are sometimes new to him. It always works, and he always expresses amazement and gratitude for the help.

When I came back from a short trip to Spokane,

Washington, where I spent joyful moments visiting with a Ponderosa pine near the river that runs through that beautiful city, the Power Tree let me know the pine had given me a message for it. As I stood near the cottonwood, opening myself to deliver the message that I didn't know I'd been carrying, I sensed encouragement and a reminder to live in the joy of the moment.

At times when I've needed an infusion of positive energy and have leaned against the cottonwood's trunk, it has shown me two tall metallic looking rods entwined around each other.

Those rods move from deep in the Earth, through my body and up to the sky in a line of unity that gives me strength. We give each other strength as our adventures with one another continue.

CHAPTER 11

BANK TREE

I protect and cleanse the land around me. I take great pride in my work.

A young juniper, the Bank Tree feels passionate about its responsibility to guard and protect the ditch bank. Even so, it is often light hearted and fun loving. It reminds me to enjoy each moment. The Bank Tree loves to be recognized and valued. It likes to be acknowledged for its dedication to duty.

The first time I met the Bank Tree, I was walking with a friend who wore Clogs. A thorn poked the bottom of his foot, and he stopped to examine the wound. The juniper had tried to attract his attention, but he'd ignored it until the thorn poked him. He asked if the tree had anything to say. The juniper told him it works diligently to oversee and protect everything along the ditch bank. So we called it the Bank Tree. This is a young tree still growing into its purpose.

The tree connected with me as well, sending what felt like a loop of energetic information flowing to my heart, up through the top of my head, and back to the tree. This is one way we and the trees share our knowledge with each other.

Though the juniper is a small tree, it has a vast, beautiful interior. It can communicate with people through its roots. That communication was once easy. Energetic pulsations in the roots created an emotional response in humans, but over time both trees and people forgot how to do it. Now we are remembering how to dialogue in this way as trust builds between us.

This young tree is so full of enthusiasm and dedication to the task of guarding the irrigation ditch bank. A friend once told me it reminds her of a buffalo, and I sense a powerful buffalo spirit is part of this tree. Even its roots that reach deep into the ground carry the etheric shape of a buffalo. That spirit sometimes presents itself as a fierce warrior and sometimes as a loving bison who rubs its head against my chest in greeting. Not only does it protect the irrigation ditch bank, but it watches out for me as well.

I often see the buffalo spirit poking its head out of the top of the tree. Sometimes it's very vigilant, and in that mode it towers over the land. At other times it offers a playful, loving or healing touch. Occasionally, it's in a deeply restful state. Once it showed me little buffalo spirits ringing the tree trunk. They represent different aspects of itself that the juniper is learning to develop. When I wonder why I'm being shown these little buffalo spirits, I sense that they represent budding aspects of the tree that it does not always recognize are there. I can relate to that. Sometimes I don't recognize the progress and the growth that I'm making, the gifts I'm developing. It often takes someone else to notice that growth and point it out to me.

Occasionally the Bank Tree needs the Father Sky, Mother Earth exercise. Instructions for this exercise may be found in the Exercise section at the end of Part 1. Depending on how much help the juniper needs, it can take up to three repetitions of the workout for the tree to forge a strong connection between Earth and God.

It is important that the tree's bond with Earth and God is strong when the buffalo spirit ferries our own unhealthy emotions through the tree and deep into the ground. There, they are transformed into something positive. Its ability to take those emotions from us and to ground them has been healing for me. When I struggle with difficulties in my life, I have felt the buffalo spirit shoulder my unhealthy emotions and give them to the Earth, which knows how to change them into healthy energy.

CHAPTER 12

BAROMETER TREE

I show you how well the trees are doing and how you are maturing.

When the Barometer Tree, a juniper, first revealed itself to me, it felt apprehensive, as though something was attacking its roots. I prayed for it and sent it Reiki, and it calmed down.

Another time, in my mind I followed the tree's roots as they moved deep into the ground. The ends of the roots looked like tendrils being electrocuted, as though they were shrieking. Across the river, a drilling rig pounded the Earth. The tree's roots began to relax when I sent them Reiki. The juniper's distress left for good when drilling activity stopped and the rig moved away.

At other times, I have seen its roots huddled together as though seeking protection. I couldn't identify what the problem was, but prayer and Reiki helped them to relax. One of its root tips seemed inflamed and sore. I didn't know why, but I called on Jesus to heal the inflammation. The next time I visited the tree, its roots looked healthy.

Over time, the juniper has shown me its roots growing deeper and deeper into the Earth. One core, central root is very powerful and grows so deep. It finds an anchor at the center of the Earth, and I often see roots expanding from it, spreading out to give the tree such a stronghold in the ground that nothing can shake it. Some of these roots sprout up to nurture me and to tell me that just as the tree is growing powerful, so am I. This often surprises me, because I don't sense much growth in myself.

When it encounters a barrier to its root growth, the Barometer Tree finds a way around it. It teaches me about perseverance and hope.

A few months after my husband died, when I visited the juniper one day, it called my attention to what looked like bowls of bark that draped themselves around my body almost like tinsel on a Christmas tree. Their purpose was to contain the strength, love and support offered to me by the trees. I felt nurtured by them during my journey through grief.

CHAPTER 13

PILLAR TREE

I offer strong background support so you can relax and enjoy the moment.

This cottonwood is like a powerful pillar, offering constant strength and support. Though a mighty and dependable force, it prefers to play a background role. Its energetic presence is far reaching, but it knows how to relax. It teaches me to enjoy the moment. I can be at ease, because it helps to protect the land and me.

Once it needed Streams of Light Energy, so I sent it that energy from God that flows down around the tree and deep into its roots, forming a protective cocoon. The exercise gave it strength. More detailed instructions on how to use that exercise are found in the Exercise section at the end of Part I.

Its frequent message to me is, "You can count on me." It is a powerful being that doesn't want to call attention to itself except to let me know it's a constant presence. It plays a huge role among the trees and with me. It helps me to stay grounded, and it provides support beyond my current ability to comprehend.

One day I came to it worried and anxious about details concerning a writing project. As I stood by its trunk and gazed into its branches, I felt laughter bubbling up through the tree. "Relax, laugh, let go of worries," it seemed to tell me. I felt lighter when I left the tree. It had reminded me in a loving way that I take myself and the issues I encounter in life much too seriously.

CHAPTER 14

WAILING TREES

Our unseen connections guide us.

On a windy April day, wailing echoed up and down the ditch as I walked beside the trees. The trunks of two tall, intertwined narrow leaf cottonwoods rubbed together, producing the sound. They seemed to model the friction that happens when two individuals collide.

The trees taught me that conflicts sometimes emanate from unresolved issues or tragedies that happened lifetimes ago. Those same people may be drawn into our lives today to give us an opportunity to heal. The original conflict may have been based on false beliefs, past programming, or misunderstandings that skewed our ability to see the truth. They may be the result of unresolved grief over the tragic death of a loved one. Something that happens in this life, perhaps the illness of a loved one or a devastating financial or other loss, may trigger fears. Those fears are likely similar to something unresolved that happened in a former life either to ourselves or someone close to us.

When those fears or grief unexpectedly overwhelm us, they may happen because in this life we meet a person we knew in a former life who played a role in the emotions that still affect us today. The jarring emotions are a way to get our attention so we can do what's necessary to find healing and wholeness. The purpose for which we came into this life could be compromised if we can't find healing, so the unsettling emotions will stay with us until we heed their call to pay attention. Unresolved conflicts and the pain that accompanies loss are not to be feared. They are opportunities to heal and grow. Hearing those two branches wail against each other was a call for me to pay attention to something in my own life that needed healing.

The Wailing Trees also remind me that when love and joy dominate our thinking, we navigate through life with more power and delight. They have a strong feminine presence. They let me know there is strength in the connections we have with others, and they remind me that unresolved issues from any life can be healed.

In spite of the strength of these trees, they sometimes need prayer. After they are prayed for, they immediately return to wholeness and balance, and they resume their roles as loving peacemakers and healers. They remind me that I can do the same.

CHAPTER 15

PEACEFUL SPIRIT TREE

When challenges arise, trust in a strength greater than your own.

A graceful narrow leaf cottonwood, the Peaceful Spirit Tree stood on the edge of the irrigation ditch bank, controlling erosion. For years it knit together a spot damaged by underground moisture due to tunneling prairie dogs. Years before, two trees near it had toppled due to erosion, creating a sadness and sense of loss in the cottonwood. In spite of its own challenges to keep well rooted and to heal its pain, the Peaceful Spirit Tree liked to help people. In striving to make them feel hopeful, peaceful and harmonious, it could briefly forget its own difficulties. Though it seldom asked anything for itself, it always loved prayer and Reiki.

The tree's energetic power center and heart formed where several forks in the tree came together. When huge cracks formed in the bank around the tree, threatening its stability, it sometimes felt overwhelmed by fear. It calmed down when I prayed, reminding it that whether the tree stood or fell, its spirit would remain alive and vital, forever connected with the Oneness of All that Is. It always felt calmer after prayer. It also drew strength from its own power center.

The cottonwood once reminded me to rest in the knowledge of who I am. Since that knowledge is often discovered at different levels of exploration, I learned to trust that no matter where my journey takes me, I am continually discovering new gems about my divine nature.

A healed wound on the Peaceful Spirit Tree's trunk marked the spot where a branch fell away long ago. People saw different patterns there. Those with emotional wounds sometimes saw a heart. Others discerned a butterfly, two profiles deep in conversation, a map or a mighty warrior.

Once when I had finished competing in a table tennis tournament in another city, I lay on the hotel room bed, exhausted. My spine felt out of alignment. Suddenly into my mind came the Peaceful Spirit Tree's healed wound, looking like two profiles communicating. "Let your masculine and feminine sides dialog equally," it seemed to say. I focused on bringing about that balance, and a wave of energy flowed through my back, easing my pain.

The eroding ditch bank eventually toppled the cottonwood, but its spirit remains alive and well. When I connect with it now, it feels light, airy, and fearless.

CHAPTER 16

SYLVIA

I spread peace, laughter, and harmony.

The friendliest of all the trees, Sylvia, an apricot tree, reminds me to be joyful, because that's where great power lies. Generous by nature, it does not feel wounded when others refuse to accept what it has to offer. It continues to offer it anyway.

Sometimes the base of Sylvia's trunk looks like a drum, and I can feel pulses of powerful drum beats coming up through its roots from deep in the Earth. Sylvia has powerful connections with the Earth.

The apricot tree first showed me that it is more than just a tree when I sensed many figures standing in its branches. They let me know they were 18 angels led by a head angel named Rosemary. As I drove out of our driveway toward town one morning, I was startled to realize that Rosemary sat in the passenger seat. She carried an air of urgency that related to the work she does. She wanted me to stay connected with her and to pay attention. I didn't know what to make of that encounter.

Two days later when I visited Sylvia, Rosemary let me know she and her angels are here to help awaken all of us, including nature, so that we can play a role in our emergence into a dimension characterized by love, joy and peace. No matter how much the angels wanted to move forward to fulfill their purpose, they couldn't unless I asked them to. I came to understand that people must command them to carry out their mission. They must have our permission. This is an awesome task. No wonder Rosemary felt so urgent when she'd sat in my car. Angels can't work on the physical plane unless we ask them to intervene. One of the meanings of the name Rosemary is an aid in remembering, and that is what she and her angels do. They help us remember how to live with each other in love, peace, harmony and balance.

When I thanked Sylvia for letting Rosemary and her 18 angels live in her branches, Sylvia filled up with joy and gratitude for being acknowledged. It's not always an easy task to carry out her purpose. Sometimes Sylvia needs prayer, though I never know what the problem is. In spite of that, the apricot tree finds great comfort and strength in prayer.

Sylvia is also home to several elementals. They are all positive beings who want what's best for everyone, including humans.

Sometimes Rosemary and her angels look like they're holding trumpets in the air and playing them in triumph. At other times, they look as though they're singing a chorus of joy. Sometimes they seem to play harps, violins or guitars as they celebrate the success of their ongoing mission.

Sylvia and her angels cheer me up and help me to stay better grounded and balanced.

Sometimes the angels in Sylvia urge me to open my heart more. They also work with a maple tree in my front yard that was less than harmonious the first time I connected with it. It complained and acted like an energetic bully. When I asked Sylvia to work with the maple tree, I was amazed at the quick and positive change in the maple. A great deal of love flows from Sylvia and from Rosemary and her 18 angels. Their purpose is all about teaching and spreading peace, joy, balance and harmony.

One day as I stood in front of Sylvia I could not feel the presence of Rosemary and her 18 angels. Their absence concerned me. They soon came back to assure me they hadn't deserted their post. They were involved in an important task somewhere else. I sent them back to their work, determined not to be so worried in the future. The next time I saw them, perched in the apricot tree, their trumpets were raised to the sky as though they were celebrating the completion of a triumphant task.

Sometimes they come down from the tree and cup me in a beautiful circle of white light. I feel nurtured and loved.

CHAPTER 17

THE GIVING TREE

Bend with the circumstances.

A narrow leaf cottonwood whose branches have curved and looped to handle challenges, the Giving Tree has discovered how to bend with the circumstances. It has learned to take life lightly, bending, adjusting and adapting to whatever happens. It lets go of anything that no longer serves it well, and the graceful beauty that results makes its branches a work of art.

When I first met this tree, I felt energy flowing from its branches into my legs and feet, then into the cottonwood's roots as they penetrated deep into the Earth. The roots connected with those of other trees that connected with still others until they created an interwoven tapestry around the globe. Speak one word, the tree seemed to say, and it travels through all our roots around the world. I feel connected with an amazing web of love and mutual support. We strengthen each other.

The Giving Tree also shows me that it can send love to others through its leaves, flowing from them like undulating waves of beautiful music that bring whatever message is needed in the moment. This seemed like an awesome gift, perhaps more awesome than the tree itself could comprehend. I prayed that the tree would recognize the value God sees in it. After that prayer, the cottonwood's leaves seemed greener, its branches more animated, and a glow of gratitude flowed from it.

Once after visiting with the Giving Tree I started to walk away, but it called me back. From several yards away I looked back at the cottonwood, taking in the gorgeous laciness of its twigs, its graceful branches reaching skyward. It just wanted me to notice.

One autumn, my husband and I had a painful decision to make about his parents, who lived in a mobile home on our property. His father needed more care than his mother or we could provide, and we made the decision to place him in a nursing home. About the same time, my husband's mother experienced recurring bouts of dizziness that no medication could help even after two visits to the emergency room. Stressed and exhausted, I visited the cottonwood. As I rested my hand on one of its curving branches, I began to sob. Its strength flowed into me. I felt knots of worry in my muscles begin to loosen. The cottonwood reminded me to bend with the circumstances, to believe that even in these challenging moments peace can be found and beauty experienced, that I am not alone, that trees will gladly help me to find peace even in the most difficult of times.

It snowed heavily one winter. Branches drooped from the weight of the snow, which froze and grew even heavier. When one branch could no longer carry the weight, it snapped off, leaving jagged pieces of bark and wood behind. Next spring, leaves sprouted from the splintered wound like hope after tragedy. Its new growth reminds me that I too can recover from wounds. I can shed old attitudes and beliefs that no longer serve me well. Letting them go means that new growth can occur.

CHAPTER 18

HEART TREE

I connect everyone together in love.

For a long time, this narrow leaf cottonwood that hid behind the Giving Tree drew my attention but wasn't ready to tell me its name. It seemed to laugh as it teased my curiosity. When it finally revealed itself as the Heart Tree, I was intrigued. It grows on a steep, brush covered hillside that plunges down toward the river. That underbrush provides shelter for smaller animals.

This nurturing tree also exudes a spirit of independence. It carries joy, delight and gratitude in all things, and it reminds me to do the same.

Sometimes when I meditate near it I feel a flow of energy coming through the top of my head, down through my heart, and into the Earth. I asked the tree once where its heart lay. It drew my attention to the base of its trunk. The heart of this tree is where its slanting trunk touches Earth.

I find myself rejuvenated when I study the beauty of its branches. They make intricate, lacy patterns against the background of the sky. When I study their intertwining, delicate designs, I forget about everything else.

CHAPTER 19

PERSEVERING TREE

What appears to be a mortal wound is only a change in circumstances.

The stump of a huge old cottonwood grips the bank across the ditch. Tree mushrooms grow at its base just above the waterline. In the fall, those mushrooms are especially beautiful.

Someone cut the tree down a few years ago, and it fell into the irrigation ditch, causing lots of work for the ditch rider and his crew, who had not authorized the cutting of that tree. Just a stump remains, but the roots continue to strengthen the ditch bank. Though deeply wounded, on some level the tree remains strong and vital.

One day the stump let me know it wasn't doing well. I prayed that angels and other non-physical helpers of trees would give it the strength it needed to carry out its purpose. I felt a huge expansion flowing from the tree. It touched me energetically to say thank you and to let me know how much stronger it felt.

The way the wood split when the tree was cut down makes it look like the stump has a mouth. Sometimes songs of joy flow from its trunk, and I can feel its happiness.

Once as I visited trees near the river, perhaps a quarter of a mile from the Persevering Tree, it followed me, its spirit untethered from its stump. It had forgotten it could travel until it decided to follow me. It loves the sense of freedom that provides.

Though it has a wonderful connection to the Earth, it had, for a time, forgotten its connection to God. As I focused on it, praying that it would reconnect with its divine nature, in my mind I saw a root-like appendage grow from the back of the stump and climb high into the air. It flowered into an etheric tree, its non-physical presence so toweringly huge that it easily rediscovered its connection with God.

It has regained its sense of laughter, which is like an act of worship for it. On some days the entire stump seems to praise God with laughter. During those times, its happiness spills over to me, and I feel renewed.

CHAPTER 20

LOVING TREE

I am stately, reliable and full of compassion.

Sitting across the river in someone's yard, this tall, graceful cottonwood has been pruned and cared for. Its trunk is painted white. It spreads branches over the land. It finds those who have experienced great loss and heartache and sends them an extra portion of love.

Sometimes I feel a circle of energy connecting us, flowing from the Loving Tree, under the river, up through my feet, out the top of my head and back to the top of the tree. In that circle, we exchange everything we know. It likes to be recognized for its power and beauty. It has a solid, rooted, practical presence.

When I send it Reiki or pray for it, the cottonwood sends gratitude and love to me. Sometimes it needs Streams of Light Energy, and it soaks it in from the tips of its roots to the top of its branches and through the entire expansion of its aura. Instructions for how to do the Streams of Light Energy exercise may be found in the Exercise section at the end of Part I.

Once when Streams of Light Energy cocooned the tree, a huge bright angel emerged from the top of its branches, spreading protection and a blessing.

When the tree feels especially big, I sense that it's picking me up in spirit and carrying me into the top of its branches so I can see from its point of view. It can travel back to the beginning of time. When I ride with it, I can access information from every time that has ever been.

If I feel stressed, the cottonwood reminds me that there is a flow to life. Cycles come and go, and all is well. It counsels me to accept love from the tree and to rest in it without trying to understand why it comes to me at certain moments. It tells me to simply rest in that love and feel renewed and fed. It likes to send an extra portion of love to people who are going through rough patches in their lives.

At times, I feel a deep pulsing coming from the cottonwood. It happens when we exchange energy and information. That sharing expands beyond us, connecting us to the divine energy and unconditional love that unites us all.

CHAPTER 21

MEDICINE TREE CLUSTER

I love to help others find balance. Life's possibilities excite me.

This cottonwood cluster has a healer's heart. Its roots have a boundless connection with universal knowledge. Through that connection they share what they know with others. They especially love to communicate with healers.

This cluster of eight trees absorbs information from people who visit and freely shares its own information, lifting people's spirits with compassion. It carries ancient wisdom. Deer like these trees and often rest under them. They like the peace, harmony and balance that the cluster provides.

The cottonwoods make it clear that they intend to help me as I do healing work with others. They want to enhance the results and to protect me from any heavy energies my clients might release.

When I stand near the trees, they balance and ground me. They remind me to breathe deeply, because breath is a good grounding tool and I balance more easily when I am well grounded. They are deeply grounded, anchoring into the center of the Earth and connecting with trees on the other side of the world. They urge me to find joy in every moment. If I focus on one particular tree in this cluster, it helps to still my chattering mind so I can relax and be in the present moment.

After I had communicated with them long enough to gain their trust, they revealed what I considered to be a treasure. I saw in my mind an image of two crossed swords over my heart, which represented the perfect balance of masculine and feminine energy. This balance creates amazing power and a connection with divine abundance. Our left brain, the male component, relies on logic and has a hard time experiencing that we all are One, part of All that Is. Our right brain, the feminine component, is where our psychic and emotional abilities live. It easily recognizes that we are all One, all connected. The two aspects of ourselves will never blend and coexist in peace and harmony until the left brain can recognize the Oneness that unites us all. Until the balance of both energies occurs, the left and right brains will stay separated, and we will not be able to experience the healing and wholeness that is possible for us. This treasure of knowledge offered by the Medicine Tree Cluster is a powerful gift.

The truth of what the cluster has taught me about left and right brain unity is not easy to learn. All of us, whether male or female, have those left and right brain attitudes within us that must come together in an understanding of the unity that flows through all of nature before we can find wholeness.

One day I felt soft energetic touches stimulating my chest. I expressed gratitude for the cluster's help, because I was having breathing challenges at that moment. As I focused on my connection with the trees, healing energy flowed into my lungs, and I breathed more deeply. When I breathe more deeply and slowly, I feel the masculine and feminine energy within me become more balanced and powerful.

Sometimes when I breathe in the energy of these cottonwoods, it feels that I am flowing in rhythm with them, and I know that these trees and I each have souls. We enrich each other as we communicate, and we expand each other's souls, becoming more than we could be without each other.

When I stand in front of the Medicine Tree Cluster, feeling sad about how more and more of the Healing Tree's branches are dying, the cottonwoods assure me that if the ancient tree can no longer fulfill its purpose, they will shoulder that responsibility. Even so, I grieve thinking about the possibility of that loss. I touch one of the cluster's leaves, and feel the tree absorb my grief by osmosis, taking it to Mother Earth, where it is transformed into reassurance that the Healing Tree will remain powerful in spirit even when its body dies.

As I spend more time with these trees, the flow of energy between us takes a different shape. Instead of a circular flow, it now takes the form of a horizontal figure eight, an infinity symbol, moving back and forth between us. Sometimes I feel it moving from side to side within me, then duplicating that side to side motion in the tree. This side to side motion is especially helpful in easing tension and dissolving the false belief that I'm not good enough.

Six months after my husband died, I still carried the grief like a heavy weight in my heart. I paid a visit to the Medicine Tree Cluster. When I touched one of its thick trunks, I felt a jolt of healing energy rush through my face and down my body into the Earth. Suddenly I felt more vigor. My heart felt lighter, my grief eased for a few moments, and I felt more alive than I had in months.

CHAPTER 22

SHIMMERING TREE

I understand my Oneness with All that Is and share that knowledge with others.

This Russian olive sat on the river's edge on someone else's land. I called it the Shimmering Tree because its branches reflected shimmering light as it bounced off the water. Not long after I met this tree, it offered me a nugget of wisdom, a treasure: the awareness of being One with the waterways of the world.

As the tree helps me to become more aware of my connection with the water, the water and I become attuned to each other's needs and the needs of the Earth. Together, we work in harmony and mutual respect to meet those needs. Part of that attunement occurs when we recognize the beauty and grandeur within each of us. When I ground myself, it's easier for me to sense my connection with the water. Sometimes it needs encouragement. At other times, it wants the removal of an energy blockage along the shore line or within the stream.

It shows me there is a way for my spirit to travel through the waterways of the entire world as the water and I help to meet each other's needs. The more I think about how to accomplish this, the less possible it seems. This is a nugget of wisdom that can't be reasoned through. It must simply be practiced with a knowing that it works.

The Shimmering Tree had its own set of needs, especially in the spring when melting snows swell the river and pound the shore. During those times, the Russian olive fears being uprooted and swept away. That's when I pray that its roots will sink deep into the Earth, holding it fast.

At times the tree has felt unsettled by something happening to its roots deep underground. At other times it feels alarmed when beavers gnaw its branches. Prayer helps the tree to relax.

One summer, the Shimmering Tree and several other Russian olives along the river were cut down as part of a federally funded program to remove them so that native trees could have more space to grow. When I learned they would soon be cut down, I let them know so they could prepare themselves. They, in turn, let me know our spirits would remain connected even when the trees were no longer in physical form. The spirit of the Shimmering Tree still lives as does the treasure it shared with me. That treasure is eternal. Nothing can damage or change it.

The spirits of the other felled Russian olives, which I named Rear Guard Tree, Companion Tree, Sucra and Hand in the Water Tree, still remain with me, reminding me that their spirits are strong and healthy.

CHAPTER 23

TEACHING TREE OR WINGS TREE

I am an enthusiastic teacher. I love to share my wisdom.

When I first encountered this cottonwood across the river from me, I felt energy from its roots traveling under the river and into my feet. From there, the energy flowed deep into the Earth. Ask for what you want, the tree seemed to say, then imagine the delight of already having it. I saw rich brown earth flowing up through my body, then traveling above my head.

As I watched, the energy turned into two fingers or branches which could hold whatever item I might request. What an amazing image to explain how to bring what I want into reality, to manifest it!

The cottonwood asked to be called the Teaching Tree, because it loves to teach others the wisdom that it carries. It was so eager to share that, early on, it sent me more than I could handle when it tried to teach me how to manifest. It didn't check to see if I had the skills necessary to receive and use the gift. The energy of what it gave me required that I know how to balance the masculine and feminine energy running through my body. Though other trees would eventually teach me how to do it, at that point I didn't have the needed skills. As a result, the energy this enthusiastic tree poured through me traumatized my unbalanced body.

I felt my abdomen in the area of my second chakra begin to ache. I was so excited to learn about what the tree was teaching me that I ignored the ache. But when I woke up the next morning, the ache was almost overwhelming. In spite of the pain, I recognized that healing and balancing were taking place. Even so, it was more than I could handle. Later in the morning I lay down in an attempt to calm my abdominal discomfort and dozed off. When I wakened, I was aware that, in spirit, two older women were standing by my feet, vigorously rubbing the balls of my feet and toes in a circular motion. I dozed off again. When I woke up, they were still rubbing my feet. I dozed off again. When I wakened, I felt a hint of relief, but the ache still felt overwhelming.

Knowing I needed help, I called my best friend, who lived 35 miles to the north. Over the phone, she offered to do a trauma energy release session with me. It's a technique that helps to release energy caught in the body due to trauma of any kind. As my friend worked with me, I sensed funnel shaped energy at the top of my head, creating a connection with God.

The wide end of the funnel fit over the top of my head. At the funnel, I saw tassels of light flowing from above my head down my body, completely covering me. The tassels then connected deep into the ground, and the aching began to ease. At the same time, I saw those tassels lift out of the ground and flow instantly to my friend even though she was 35 miles away. The lights from those tassels formed a tender, protective cocoon around her. She faced difficulties of her own. As I watched, a beautiful white angel emerged from the cocoon, knelt beside my friend and wrapped comforting, encouraging arms around her.

The core of this energy movement involves tassels or streams of protective, nurturing light flowing from God, through the top of a person's head, into their body, and anchoring them deep into the Earth. Then the Earth sends its own nurturing energy back through the person's body, reconnecting it with God. I called it Streams of Light Energy. Once I learned it, many trees asked me for it. I found it to be an effective grounding and healing tool. Trees love to receive it. It helps them to remember they are connected to both the Earth and to God's divine presence.

I thanked the Teaching Tree for giving me this gift, which helped me to recover from the trauma of learning too much before I was ready. Once I recovered, I felt more energized and healthy than I'd felt in a long time. I also understood that this tree has the ability to travel anywhere and to be with me whenever I need it.

At another time, the Teaching Tree seemed to touch my solar plexus, remove it, sew up a tear in the top of it, and replace it in my body. The tear made it harder for my solar plexus and heart chakras to work together. When the repair was completed, communication between those two chakras improved.

Once, I and the friend, who could send the energy of water where it was needed, stood near the Teaching Tree. I saw in my mind an arrow moving from my head to his heart and another one moving from my heart to his head. I didn't understand what I was seeing and expressed my confusion. In an effort to help, my friend came up with his own interpretation of what the arrows meant.

It wasn't until the next morning that I saw the complete picture of what the tree was trying to show me. Instead of the one-way arrows I had seen the night before, I saw two-way arrows, indicating the flow of energy from my head to my friend's heart and back from his heart to my head. The other arrow flowed from my heart to his head and back from his head to my heart. I was seeing a picture of the perfect balance of masculine and feminine energy. It's a lesson several trees have taught me as I strive to learn how to keep these energies balanced. On another level, it also contains an image of how we are all One, how we help to balance each other as we recognize that all of us are connected.

One fall day, as I stood admiring the cottonwood's yellowing leaves, I felt energy hurtling from the tree to my heart. Suddenly, the energy slowed down, and I could almost hear the tree say, "Oops!" as it remembered not to overpower me. The message was clear. Notice not only the beauty of changing leaf colors in the fall, but notice every experience through the eyes of my heart. Experiencing beauty through the heart helps me to stay focused without the intrusion of other thoughts while I immerse myself in the glorious gifts that nature has to offer. When we keep our hearts balanced, we can see everything more clearly.

This ability to stay focused also helps the trees. Sometimes they just need my undivided attention while I acknowledge and appreciate them. That recognition gives them strength.

Much later, I met two women who liked to walk along the irrigation ditch bank and visit the river. As I got to know them and recognized their love for nature, it seemed appropriate to tell them about the trees. When I asked the Teaching Tree if that would be all right, I could feel its excitement. Both women immediately bonded with many of the trees, prayed for them and sent them love. When they needed encouragement, the trees offered it to them.

Four years after I first met the Teaching Tree, it let me know it wanted a different name. I focused on the tree, trying to understand what that name was, but I couldn't figure it out. A yellow butterfly flitted around the tree. I could almost see the tree jumping up and down in an attempt to get my attention. Perhaps, I thought, it wants to be called the butterfly tree. There was no confirming response from the tree. As I struggled to find the right name, the tree kept telling me, "Look at me, look at my shape." Bushy branches on the bottom half of the tree reminded me of a set of wings, and its upper branches seemed to form another set of wings. Finally I understood. "You're the Wings Tree!" I exclaimed, and it bubbled with energetic joy.

When I began my shamanic training, the Wings Tree showed me where to find one of the stones that would represent the south direction in my medicine bundle. The stone looks a little bit like a set of wings.

On another day the cottonwood told me that its winged shape helps me to remember that I can fly wing to wing with

God as I fulfill my purpose. Later, I learned that the butterfly is a symbol of transformation. Perhaps the Wings Tree is letting me know it too symbolizes transformation.

CHAPTER 24

WRITING TREES CLUSTER

We help others fulfill their dreams.

Across the river, this cluster of cottonwoods lines the bank. When I send Reiki to the cluster, it sparkles with energy. I call them the Writing Trees Cluster because I feel their support when I work on writing projects. Sometimes the energy of their encouragement feels like it's flowing out of my hands and feet. At other times I feel it strengthening my solar plexus.

When I first connected with these trees, they were afraid they would be cut down. Most trees carry this fear, but it grows smaller when people acknowledge them and thank God for them. When I asked angels to surround the trees and keep them safe, the cluster began to relax.

One day the trees asked for prayer because their roots were absorbing something toxic. I prayed that their roots would be protected from anything toxic and that they would draw from the ground only nourishment to keep them healthy and strong. They responded instantly to prayer, and they felt encouraged and safe. It was another reminder to me that prayer is a powerful tool.

When I thank the cluster of cottonwoods for the help they provide, I feel their energetic presence fill me with joy. They love to be acknowledged.

CHAPTER 25

JOYFUL TREE

With encouragement, I spread joy.

Early on, this cottonwood near the riverbank worried that I would not continue to visit it. It wasn't sure it could trust me, so I started calling it the Worry Tree. It wanted to be sure I would visit even during cold winter months when snow lay on the ground.

After many visits, trust developed between us. Because it felt joyful every time it saw me, I renamed it the Joyful Tree. Its branches almost look like hands lifting in praise to God because the tree feels so joyful.

For three years I wasn't able to get close to the cottonwood because a plethora of Russian olive trees surrounded it. After a federal program provided money to remove the Russian olives so that native trees could have more space to grow, I was able to touch the Joyful Tree's trunk. It looked different than I thought it would. Two trunks grew so close together they looked as though they came from the same root. A third trunk a few feet away formed the top part of the tree, which was all I could see when Russian olives had crowded around it. I walked to each trunk and touched it. Joy billowed from the tree. Its name fits it well.

When I was preparing for my first Shamanic workshop, in which we explored the south direction, the Joyful Tree pointed out a nearby rock it wanted to be in my mesa, or medicine bundle. The trees have been involved and generous in my shamanic training.

CHAPTER 26

PROTECTOR TREES

We protect people from the painful aspects of life by sprinkling hope.

A set of three cottonwoods on the far side of the river stands guard protectively along the bank. I call them the Protector Trees because they make me feel safe no matter what happens in my life.

When the trees' roots feel stressed from underground activity or from spring flood water that undermines their roots, they ask for prayer. When I pray for them, they feel calmer.

Sometimes I feel them connecting with me from under the river and up through the ground into my feet. Their energy feels gentle but powerful. One day I felt it strongly at my throat, and it undulated through my neck, helping the muscles to relax and any misalignment to heal. After a few minutes, the energy flow changed. It formed a circle between the trees and me, moving from the top of my head to the top of the cottonwoods' branches, down their trunks, under the water, up through the soil, into my feet, up through my body and out through the top of my head to begin the circle with the tree all over again. I have come to recognize this movement as the way we exchange information.

Another day I felt them strengthening my solar plexus, helping me to feel powerful. I let my voice lift in praise to God, and they responded with such a depth of joy that I felt even more powerful.

CHAPTER 27

DANCING TREE

Celebrate the joy of life by dancing.

This elm across the river loves to dance. For several months after I met it, the tree felt weakness at its roots and often asked for Reiki, Streams of Light Energy and prayer. It stands near an oil and gas well site. In spite of that challenge, the tree no longer needs much attention. It seems to have found its balance.

One day a friend felt shattered after an unsettling visit in Germany with her mother. She spent a few hours with me. I took her down to the trees, and the Dancing Tree immediately started sending energy to her. The elm encouraged her to dance and to spend more time playing.

My friend's spirits revived, and she felt refreshed when she left. She gifted me with a music box angel called *Schutzengel*, meaning angel guardian, that she had purchased in Germany. When we walked across the irrigation ditch bridge to go back to the house, I noticed for the first time that a large angel stood by the bridge. I called him Schutzengel, and he has been there ever since, a faithful guardian.

One November afternoon, the Dancing Tree wanted my attention. As I focused on it, I found myself caught up in a whirling dance with it as we cavorted through the sky. We moved so freely that we both felt giddy with delight. It's a freedom that comes from letting go of everything that's negative or judgmental, putting our awareness instead on the joy of being in the moment. This method helps both the tree and me to transform sadness, worry, anger, confusion, and any other negative emotion into something worth celebrating.

When I struggle to find the time to meet my own needs while not neglecting people who are close to me, the Dancing Tree tells me, "Be still in your mind. Be still in your body. Be still and know." In that moment, where there is no past, no future, no loss, no gain, no fear, everything becomes a celebration of life. That's cause for dancing!

CHAPTER 28

BEAUTY TREE

I help you remember how powerful you are.

This huge cottonwood across the river reminds me that I am more powerful than I think I am. For a while I could not grasp the concept, because I didn't feel powerful at all.

The Beauty Tree showed me an image of myself as a giant, my knees touching the top of the cottonwood, my head bent down to peer into its uppermost branches. The Beauty Tree reminds me that I still don't understand how powerful I am, but it assures me that I'm learning. One by-product of hanging out with the trees is feeling more self-confident!

On some days, there's an urgency to the cottonwood's message: "Stop hiding and walk as the powerful being you are. Let go of judgment. Radiate joy. The Earth needs that now!" This letting go of judgment isn't easy. I often fall into old thinking patterns, but the Beauty Tree applauds my progress.

Many years ago, when I had to give up a passionate but financially unsuccessful line of work for a job that helped to feed my family, I struggled with grief. I felt like a derailed train, no longer following my life's purpose. Much later I was able to return to that passion, but some of the grief remained stuck in my body. One day the Beauty Tree sent me a huge wave of love and taught me an exercise to release my grief. I call it the Breath of Love.

The cottonwood instructed me to breathe in deeply, letting my ribs expand. As I breathe out, I am to imagine the grief flowing out from both sides of my ribs. As it releases, the air dilutes it, and all of nature helps to soak in the grief and ground it so it can be transformed into something positive.

As I practiced this form of breathing, I realized that grief was not only spilling out from my ribs but coming from the front and back of my torso as well. My breath, the tree explained, is coming in through my heart and out through all sides of my ribs. As I breathe in, I am breathing in love from all affectionate beings alive today, no matter how microscopic or colossal they may be. As I breathe out, that love helps to flush away the grief. I am staggered by the enormity of nature's generous gift to me.

When I first tried the exercise, it felt like my grief could find no escape. But as I kept trying, my rib cage began to soften. In my mind's eye, I could see wisps of grief escape from small holes between my ribs.

Over a period of several days, the activities of a drilling rig near the river left many trees' roots feeling traumatized. I prayed for them and sent them Reiki to help them navigate the challenge more easily. When the drilling rig finally left, the Beauty Tree thanked me for helping all the trees through those difficult times. Its own mood brightened after the rig was gone.

When the cottonwood asks me to focus on it, I see how gigantic this tree really is. Its non-physical form shoots high into the sky, and it can find me anywhere I may be on the planet.

No matter where it goes, it sends positive vibrations to help everyone recognize their true potential and their purpose. This activity brings it great joy.

It helps me to see an oval connection forming between Earth and sky as the trees and I practice the Mother Earth/Father Sky exercise. Find more detailed instructions for how to do this exercise in the Exercise section at the end of Part I. An oval pathway of black and gold creates a constant loop within the structure of the tree or me. As the energy flows within that oval pathway, it removes negative energy that can form blockages in my body or within the trees. The more I practice that exercise, the clearer I become.

During my shamanic training, the Beauty Tree wanted to contribute a stone for my medicine bundle. It provided the resistance stone, one that helps to overcome our resistance to positive change and healing. As I walked along the riverbank opposite the Beauty Tree, I kept my eyes to the ground, searching for the stone I knew was waiting for me. At a steep area of the bank, where rocks had formed a sort of stairway down to the water, I spotted the stone. It was cream colored, almost white, and it stood out from every other rock in that area. Gingerly, I stepped my way down to the water and picked it up. Since then, I have used it several times when I've faced challenges that felt too difficult for me.

CHAPTER 29

JOSEPHINE

I remind you to rest.

Josephine, a cottonwood, leafs later in the spring than most other cottonwoods. It feels strong and powerful to me. Once in mid-December I asked her to tell me what was true about her in that moment. She replied, "Rest." She was resting when it was time to rest. Rest is something we all need in order to keep ourselves healthy. It is not a luxury. It is a necessity. We should not feel selfish or unproductive to rest when our bodies need rest to recuperate. When we are rested, we are more able to be productive.

A month-and-a-half after my mother died, I visited Josephine and felt grief that I thought was coming from the tree. The cottonwood let me know I wasn't feeling her grief; I was feeling my own grief. As I focused on what she had to teach me, I could feel the grief flowing from my heart down my body and through my feet into the ground.

"Blow it out," she seemed to say. "Push it out through your feet." I began doing that, and with the extra effort of blowing it out through my feet, I sensed more and more of it releasing into the ground. I thanked Josephine for showing me another way to handle grief.

CHAPTER 30

RAHAB

I connect with a reservoir that holds the knowledge of Mother Earth.

Sometimes when I think of Rahab, I see beneath her a vast chamber that looks empty. Rahab assures me I am seeing something non-physical, a reservoir of the Earth's knowledge. It is not empty. Instead it holds a wealth of wisdom that can be grasped by that intuitive part of ourselves that sees beyond any of our five senses.

One February day, I sensed a sadness in Rahab. Though she assured me she was okay, I asked God to help her sense joy.

Immediately, I felt joy burst through her trunk and branches. Her instantaneous response reminded me of how powerful and effective prayer is.

On an early spring day, Rahab asked me to take a picture of its three trunks that look solidly anchored to the ground, so I did. Those trunks look powerful and capable of connecting to a vast reservoir of knowledge.

CHAPTER 31

PEARL

I am solidly grounded, and my presence brings healing.

Pearl is a young elm that helps to ground those nearby. The tree's essence promotes healing. When you feel the need for physical or emotional nurturing, stand under an elm and enjoy its healing presence. Once when my lungs felt stressed, I touched Pearl's trunk. My chest began to expand, and my breathing eased.

Pearl likes to share its knowledge and to have us share with it what we know. That sharing feels like a circle of energy moving up through my body, into the treetop, down through its roots, into the Earth, and up through my feet in a continuous circle. This circle also helps to give us a boost of energy and encouragement when we need it.

In spite of its youth, Pearl grows among trees that form a line from the Healing Tree down through the fields and across the river to the Teaching Tree, also known as Wings. These trees have agreed to take on the Healing Tree's tasks when the cottonwood can no longer shoulder them. The Medicine Tree Cluster, which is in this line of trees, has also agreed to take on that extra responsibility when necessary. I'm grateful to witness how incredibly supportive trees are of each other. They form a community, and they work together in harmony.

CHAPTER 32

RUTH TREE

I like to follow those who connect with me. I am a quiet supporter of many.

An elm, the Ruth Tree often has little to say, but its quiet heart-to-heart connection feels welcoming and loving. At other times, its energy moves through me from the ground up, blossoming toward the sky in a burst of health. That movement has a healing quality, and it helps me to stay grounded.

Early on, when I stood near the tree I often felt the need to do the Father Sky, Mother Earth exercise, strengthening the elm's connection with both Earth and sky. At first I thought the tree needed that exercise. Now I suspect it asked for the exercise because I needed it. Learn more about this exercise in the Exercise section at the end of Part I.

Practicing that exercise also helped the elm learn that it could trust having an interaction with humans. Trees everywhere are learning how to reestablish that trust. It grows as we respect and appreciate each other.

After I had known this tree for a few months, I could tell the level of trust was rising because the elm often told me when it needed prayer. After I prayed for it, I could feel its strength and confidence grow. Gradually, it began to feel so calm and peaceful, and its requests for prayer dwindled. When I asked why it seldom asked for prayer anymore, it explained that because it knows it can trust me it no longer needs to test my willingness to help. It often likes to travel with me. I love knowing that its non-physical presence spends so much time with me.

Ruth has one large trunk and a smaller one. I admired its large trunk one day and told the elm how beautiful it looks. In a matter of fact way, it replied, "I know. I'm glad you noticed."

CHAPTER 33

TRUMPET TREE

I remind others to focus on their purpose, for it will give them direction.

When I first noticed this cottonwood on a neighbor's property, its branches reminded me of the shape of a trumpet raised in the air, providing music for everyone. It liked the name trumpet, so I called it the Trumpet Tree. About a year later tragedy struck it.

Badly damaged in a neighbor's out-of-control brush fire, the Trumpet Tree struggled to return to health. In spite of its gallant effort to live, it finally died, but its spirit remains strong.

During its struggle to survive, I used to do the Father Sky, Mother Earth exercise with it because it made the tree feel more hopeful. Learn more about this exercise in the Exercise section at the end of Part I. I also sent it Reiki and prayed for it. When I spend time with this tree and another cottonwood beside it that was also badly damaged in the fire, I can feel the joyful gratitude of nearby trees. They love to see other trees get needed help.

Recently, the Trumpet Tree's spirit drew my attention to many small pieces of wood on the ground that had fallen from it. Those small but sturdy strips made excellent pendulums. I use them in my healing work. I feel grateful when I remember how the Trumpet Tree gifted me with those pieces of itself.

CHAPTER 34

LIGHT FINGERS TREE

I am a healer, and I share my healing tools.

When I first made contact with this cottonwood in our front yard, it revealed a loving spirit. It taught me how to ground better. As I felt its energy flow from my head down through my body, I could feel blockages at my upper legs, knees and ankles, but they soon disappeared. When I asked the cottonwood how I can stay better grounded, it told me, "Love the ground."

Besides being a healer, it likes to share its knowledge. It showed me how to let healing energy flow through my heart, then move down my arms into my fingers and how to let my fingers grow very long. It helped me understood that my fingers have a limitless reach and are free of the restraints of time and space. They can even extend across galaxies if the need arises. The left hand receives healing energy from God while the right hand probes to discover needy areas, then delivers energy there.

It showed me how my extended fingers can dissolve energy blockages. As healing energy flows from God through my heart, down my arms and into my fingers, that energy helps to calm and relax people and elements in nature so they can begin to heal.

I learned from the cottonwood that my extended fingers will find some areas that need to be stimulated and other areas that need to be sedated so that healing can occur most effectively. "I will help you in your healing work," the tree told me one day. I sensed my Oneness with it, and I felt lovingly supported.

CHAPTER 35

MAPLE TREE

I am a worrier, but I am learning to feel more peaceful.

The first time I sat under this tree and paid close attention to it, great love flowed from it to me. It revealed a tendency to worry by drawing attention to small rust marks on its trunk made by the lawn sprinkler. When I asked the tree if it would be willing to receive Reiki, it replied with a longing yes, as though it wondered why I hadn't asked before. It pointed to its roots as one place it especially needed Reiki.

When I sent it Reiki a few days later, it received the energy with ease. A few weeks later, however, its attitude changed. It didn't seem to benefit from the Reiki I sent it that day, so I sent it Streams of Light Energy instead. When two streams of energy flowed from God, through my head and toward the top of the tree, the maple snatched them. It wrapped them around itself like a teasing pre-teen might do after swiping a hat from someone's head. The maple didn't absorb the energy from the exercise and after a couple of hours it tossed the energy away.

The next day during a period of meditation, I sensed that the maple's teasing behavior, which bordered on bullying, comes from a deep seated fear that its needs will not be met and that it will not survive. So I asked the Twinkling Lights Tree to work with it. In my mind's eye, I saw the cottonwood's branches sprinkle twinkling lights of energy all over the maple tree. After that, the maple's attitude started to change. It began to trust me a little more. As time went on, it even began to feel joyful.

Later, Sylvia worked with the maple as well and helped it to embrace a more peaceful, harmonious attitude. Now sometimes the maple sends me a wave of love, and its trust level has increased. It has a deep connection with the planet as well as with the divine. The maple has improved more than any other tree I've met, thanks in large part to the intervention of other trees.

CHAPTER 36

SENTINEL TREES

Demi Gavotto Ron Asanji Samson

My husband and I planted this row of five Austrian pines in 1974, shortly after we bought the house in which I lived for 42 years. They were only a foot tall then. Today they tower more than 20 feet into the air. They are sentinels who watch over us and our property. Each has its own name and takes pride in its responsibilities.

Samson

I am a caring protector. I love to help you in your healing work.

Though it is an austere tree, it sends me great love. It is the pine tree closest to the county road in front of our house. It carries an air of leadership. It keeps an eye on other trees on and near our property and offers protection, support, and strength.

After I taught a Reiki I workshop and passed the attunement to my students, one pupil felt over-stimulated with buzzing energy. I took the women outside and asked Samson if my student could share some of her excess energy with the tree. So much joy burst from the pine! Until then, I hadn't realized how much it wanted to help. My student felt relief as soon as she touched one of Samson's branches.

This tree sends me an abundance of love. It sometimes asks for prayer. I never know what problems it faces, but it always feels stronger after prayer.

When I get a treatment from the naturopathic healer who can see through the veil, Samson sometimes shows up to help. Once when I was spraying the lawn and trees with an organic product meant to stimulate and support growth, I could feel an excited pull coming from Samson and the other sentinel trees.

They could hardly wait to be sprayed.

Asanji

I am light hearted laughter. I focus on the positive.

Though weakened several years ago by bark beetles, it has bounced back and bristles with new growth in its upper branches. Even before it let me know its name, it sent me lots of love and asked me to touch its branches. Touch is one way in which we exchange energy.

Ron

I thrive on challenges.

Ron does not communicate much but is an alert sentinel. It has an amazingly strong connection between the Earth and God. Over the years, some trees forgot that connection, but they all seem to have relearned it. Ron is a master at maintaining that relationship.

Gavotto

I absorb negative emotions and unhealthy environmental influences.

Gavotto, with a soft sound like a "j", has told me little about itself. It lost several branches to a bark beetle infestation but is recovering. It likes me to notice how big and beautiful it is in spite of its challenges. Gavotto was the last of the five sentinel trees to tell me its name. Once I knew all their names, the trees exuded an extra burst of joy.

Demi

I love to nurture others.

Short for Demetria, this tree is taller than any of the others. It is proud of its beauty and is willing to share its shade.

After some representatives of the electric power company came to our house to tell us that Demi's branches would have to be trimmed because they grew into the power lines, I told the pine what to expect. Demi seemed fearful, afraid that she would be cut down. I asked the Healing Tree to teach her how to handle the trimming. The Healing Tree had once successfully used deep grounding techniques to survive when some of its large branches were cut off. Whatever the cottonwood said to Demi, it worked, because the pine survived the trimming well and with no trauma that I can discern.

Sometimes I thank Demi for the shade she provides over our propane tank. Demi likes to be acknowledged and appreciated.

CHAPTER 37

LEYVON TREE CLUSTER

If people observe my branches in a meditative state, I help to heal their emotional hurts.

Well-grounded to Earth and sky, this elm is a healer. It helps to remove negative energy that can cause inflammation and, if unchecked, lead to physical illness. The tree showed me how it accomplishes this and let me know I could do it too. I imagine a counterclockwise circle of energy moving over someone's head. When that energy creates enough suction, in my mind I see what looks like little seeds popping out of people's heads almost like popcorn as the inflammation is released.

As with almost every tree, the Leyvon Cluster likes to be acknowledged and recognized for what it has to offer. When people take time to appreciate it, the elm loves the Oneness that forms between them.

CHAPTER 38

THE RIVER

I am strong and harbor great truths, many of which are still waiting to be discovered.

I feel peaceful when I stand by the river near our home. I didn't know a deeper connection with it was possible until my friend, who can send the energy of water, asked me to see its spirit. The question surprised me. How could I see something that wasn't in physical form? Out of curiosity, I focused my attention and almost immediately saw in my mind what looked like three large triangles of water. Each triangle had another triangle for a head. They formed three triangular figures with triangular heads. They skipped across the river's surface, looking playful and happy. Surprised, I wondered if I'd imagined it, but it seemed genuine. The river's triangular spirit bodies have popped up on the river at other times as well.

Not long after I recognized that I had a deeper connection with the river, I was looking north along the river when I felt its anger. As I tried to understand the problem, the river let me know that three people, two adults and a child who had died about 250 years ago, never crossed over to the light. Instead, they remained near what had been a holy place to them while they were in human form. This holy place had long ago washed away, but the spirits continued to guard where it once stood. They built energetic obstructions in the river to keep the water away from it. Those dams created an energy blockage in the river. The water kept washing it away in an attempt to free itself of the block. The spirits built it back up, determined to carry out their holy duty. This frustrated the river and made it angry. I focused on a recent obstruction the spirits had built, and it disintegrated so easily that I was startled. It was so easy to remove the blockage, yet I'd had no idea I could do such things by willing them to be gone.

The spirits who hadn't yet crossed over didn't know their efforts were having a negative effect on the river. When I asked them if they wanted Reiki, I could feel their desire for it. As I sent them Reiki, I told them it was time for them to cross over to the light. I asked angels to help them make that transition. A portal of light appeared near them. The two adult spirits immediately crossed over, but the child spirit could not.

It explained it was carrying the guilt of many people, and it had to stay here to shoulder that burden. This false belief kept the child anchored to Earth. When the child understood that the guilt it thought it carried had long ago dissolved and was never meant for it to bear, it zipped through the portal to the other side.

After that, hundreds of earthbound spirits found their way to the other side through the portal. Another portal soon joined it, and they remain by the river so other earthbound spirits can find their way to the other side.

These days the river flows smoothly most of the time with no energetic obstructions.

When I sense that obstructions exist, I pray for the river, focus on the obstructions and watch them crumble. Sometimes I use what I call the White Light Cleanse. I send white light to wherever I sense an obstruction. To me, that light represents God's unconditional love. As the light finds the obstruction, it absorbs anything negative so that it dissolves and dissipates. I also send the white light through the river and along both banks to absorb any energy blockage or discord I may not have noticed. Afterwards, the river feels sparkling clean and flows with greater ease. Find the White Light Cleanse in the Exercise section at the end of Part I.

When the river feels playful, it shows me its spirit like a huge energetic water spout.

Sometimes it feels sad and needy. At those times, it needs me to be aware of it, to sense my Oneness with it, and to pray for it. When I do that, its sadness soon vanishes.

The river holds a treasure of gifts. Once it showed me an image of a treasure box sitting in the middle of the stream. The lid opened, and inside the box was an endless supply of multi-colored keys. As I watched, one key floated from the box through the air to my heart. I felt the key's energetic form unlock access to every part of my heart so that nothing remained dormant or unused.

Several months later, another key unlocked my throat, which has been an area of weakness for me. Not only has it been hard for me to clearly state what I'm thinking and feeling and to choose what I really want to do, I've also had thyroid issues there. In addition, when I eat something I'm allergic to, I start to lose my voice. The key went to my throat, and my throat began to feel stronger and more powerful. My throat reminded me that now I can cultivate that part of myself without fear.

At another time, the treasure chest in the river provided me with a key to forgiveness. This key allows me to cut the cords between me and anyone who I have trouble forgiving or who holds a grudge against me. Once the cords are cut, there are no cords through which my energy can drain to the other person. I no longer feel energetically tied to the person or issue. This gift helps me find a remarkable sense of wholeness and freedom. As I exercise that gift, I realize that all of nature, including humans, can forgive and find wholeness more easily because of the river's gift.

Once when my dog went walking along the river with me, then ran off to play somewhere, I worried about her safety. I searched for her up and down the river but couldn't find her. My anxiety skyrocketed. Would she hurt herself, bother others, be picked up by someone who would mistreat her? In the middle of my turmoil, out of the treasure box in the river came two keys that settled on my shoulders. Calm and peace cloaked me, and I even felt a hint of joy. I went back to the house, and within a few hours my dog returned from her adventure with a huge smile on her face.

On another day, the river invited me to put a key into the treasure box, so I deposited one filled with love. Other people, as well as wild animals who live on and near the river, have also deposited wonderful keys into the river's treasure box, providing an unending supply.

During a time when I tried especially hard to let go of judgment, I asked the river if it could help me reach my goal. Immediately, my eyes were drawn to thousands of stones that lined the edge of the river. I understood they were all equally important and valued. To find fault with any of them would be incredibly senseless.

The river teaches me that we work best together when I become aware of my Oneness with it. A way I can sense that Oneness is to imagine my breath mingling with the spirit of the river. Sometimes I sense an endless loop connecting us as we share what we know. Once while we were in this spirit of Oneness, I asked the river to take peace, harmony and balance wherever it traveled on its journey as it merged with streams, eddies, lakes and oceans around the world. My heart leaped as I felt the river's joy.

CHAPTER 39

EXERCISES

FATHER SKY/MOTHER EARTH EXERCISE

The Father Sky / Mother Earth exercise helps to remind us all of our connection to God and Earth, to the physical and non-physical realms.

Imagine a golden light representing God's unconditional love flowing from above the top of the tree, through its trunk, branches and leaves and deep into the Earth. See the light forming a continuous circle that connects the tree with sky and Earth. Let it flow as long as the tree seems to need it.

After you do this exercise for a while, you may notice an oval loop flowing within the tree itself. It never leaves its black and gold pathway inside the tree: black for the rich nourishment of the Earth and gold for the light of God's love. This exercise helps the tree to remember its connection to God and Earth.

You can also practice this exercise on yourself. Imagine golden light flowing from God through the top of your head, connecting you with the ground, then drawing from the Earth all that's nourishing and nurturing and letting it flow through you back up to God.

The more you practice this with the trees or with yourself, the easier it will be for you and the trees to dissolve internal energetic blockages.

STREAMS OF LIGHT ENERGY

When the Teaching Tree first showed me this exercise, I

saw it as tassels, or ribbons, of white light flowing from God through the top of a person or tree. The tassels surrounded the tree or person and grounded them deep into the Earth.

Sometimes emerging out of those tassels will come images, such as a kneeling angel, to help me better understand what the person or tree needs. The more I used the exercise, the more the tassels took on the image of light itself, full of unconditional love.

I use a form of this exercise at the beginning of a Reiki session if my client is not well grounded. I ask the person to visualize a white light flowing from God through the top of their head, completely surrounding them and grounding them deep into the Earth. Then I ask them to see that light flowing from the nourishing, nurturing Earth through and around their bodies, protecting them and reconnecting them with God.

Practice it often to feel the love and protection of God surrounding you.

WHITE LIGHT CLEANSE

When you sense darkness around a person, tree, river, or other element of nature, the White Light Cleanse can help you dissolve that darkness.

The first time I used it, I sensed a dark, murky energetic presence, like an obstruction, in the river. So I sent the white light of God's unconditional love down the river and onto both banks. The light absorbed anything negative. Everything that is not part of God's unconditional love dissolves and dissipates in the light of that love. After I did that exercise, energetic murkiness left the river, and it felt clear again.

Practice this exercise when you are out in nature so you get a better sense of how it works before you try it in more challenging situations. Nature delights in helping us to learn the technique. Call on Archangel Michael and his band of angels to remove any darkness that persists.

BREATH OF LOVE

This exercise is especially helpful with grief, but can be used for any feeling that troubles you. Imagine that you are breathing love into your heart. After you feel much love fill your heart, breathe out through your ribs. Imagine that whatever feeling you need to release is flowing from you with each out breath.

If it feels like nothing is releasing, don't despair. Breathe in again, filling your heart with love. Then breathe out again through your ribs. If you do this a few times, you will notice that your ribs seem to soften. Soon you will see a small channel on each side of your ribs. Through that channel will flow part of what you want to release.

You may need to do this exercise several times over several days to release everything that you want to let go of. Do this exercise whenever you feel stress, grief, anger, worry, fear, or other emotion that no longer serves you well.

BALANCING ENERGY

One of the more challenging tasks I've found is to balance the masculine and feminine energy, the yin and yang, the being and doing aspects of your self. A simple technique is to imagine an old fashioned scale with a tray on each side. On one tray put your masculine energy.

On the other tray put your feminine energy. Watch the scale until the two trays balance. Once those scales are balanced, the energy within yourself is balanced. You may need to do this exercise several times a day until it becomes second nature.

CIRCLE OF KNOWLEDGE

Trees want to exchange knowledge with us. When I come home from a trip, they sometimes use this exercise to discover what I've learned and to receive messages that trees in other parts of the country want to share with them. I seldom know that I have messages for the trees until I feel drawn to touch their trunks and spend extra time with them. In those moments, I become aware of a circle of energy flowing between us that contains messages from other trees. The messages are always positive and often full of encouragement.

The circle of energy usually begins by moving downward from the tree, through its roots, into the ground, up through my feet into my body. Then it spills out of the top of my head to the uppermost branches of the tree. From there, it flows down through the trunk and roots to begin the circle all over again. In that process, we exchange everything we know.

To practice this exercise, stand near a tree with which you have developed a connection. Acknowledge it. Thank it for itself. Then let it know you want to exchange information. Focus on imagining a circle connecting you. Enjoy the unity, compassion and mutual respect that accompanies that connection. You may have flashes of insight that help you glimpse bits of what you and the tree have shared. At other times you will simply feel a greater sense of wellbeing.

REMOVING NEGATIVE ENERGY

To remove negative energy from anything, including yourself, see a huge counterclockwise semi-circle traveling from your left foot following the left side of your body up to the left side of your head. Once it reaches the middle of your head, send it plunging down through the center of your body to your feet.

When it gets to your toes, send it in a clockwise semi-circular motion from your right foot, following the right side of your body, back up to the right side of your head. Once it reaches the center of your head, again send it down through the middle of your body to your feet, where it will start a counterclockwise circle traveling up the left side of your body to your head. There, it will plunge from your head down through your body to your feet and begin a clockwise circle from your right foot up to the top of your head. Keep this circular loop going as long as it feels necessary.

This vigorous movement of energy clears false beliefs and past programming that no longer serve you well. It fills the vacated space with positive energy that is better suited for you at this time.

PART II

A WEALTH OF TOOLS

INTRODUCTION

When I visited the Twinkling Lights/Power Tree one day, on its trunk I saw eleven blue dots connected by red lines in a rough oval shape. It reminded me of a road map between stars. Eventually, I came to understand that each dot represented a category of tools, and each category contained ten different tools. The lines between each dot showed a natural progression from one set of tools to another.

Over a period of three years, eleven categories, each containing 10 non-physical tools, were revealed to me. The tools were remarkable, and the categories often surprised me. Learning to use each tool effectively takes practice, and I will never learn to master all of them. The large number of tools makes it easier to pick and choose which ones resonate with you as you use them. A few tools involve such key concepts that they appear in more than one category. Among them are tools for staying grounded, expressing gratitude and giving and receiving love.

Because you can't hold the tools in your hand, they must be used with the mind and heart. That may bring up all sorts of red flags in some people's minds. Is this a hoax? Is it a case of imagination gone wild? Is there any truth to the tools at all? Maybe there's a con artist at work here like the criminals who fooled many people in *The Emperor's New Clothes.*

In that story, an emperor is deceived by two rogues who convince him they can weave special material that's invisible to idiots. The emperor's competent officials can't see the material, but they're afraid to say anything because they don't want to be called idiots. So they pay the rogues a handsome fee for the invisible cloth out of which others create invisible clothes because they don't want to be branded as idiots either. The emperor can't see the clothes, but he's also afraid people will think he's an idiot, so he parades down the street in the non-existent clothes that everyone assures him are magnificent. Not until an innocent child points out that the emperor is naked do people snap out of their fear and realize they've been duped.

Have I too been duped? Have I convinced myself the tools are real when they're not? Early on as the tools revealed themselves to me while I meditated near the tree, I asked myself those questions. Whenever I sought divine guidance, I always came away feeling that the tools were genuine. You will have to make up your own mind about that.

If you're interested in experimenting with the tools, I suggest you pick one category and try a few tools that appeal to you. It's not necessary to use every tool. Move onto another category when you're ready. If one category doesn't hold your interest, skip it.

As each tool introduced itself to me, it sometimes came with a description that related to challenges I faced in my life at that time. Had the tools been revealed to others, the descriptions would have been different, tailored to their own unique experiences. This is the nature of connecting with our Inner Self, our broader connection with the divine nature of God. We tap into our own unique set of experiences to shape our understanding. When I communicate with trees, I am speaking heart to heart with them and tapping into my own Inner Wisdom, into that divine part of myself that connects us all. That divinity is all about loving, nurturing and healing. It is most accessible on a heart to heart level. From that place of unconditional love, I have come to trust the trees, and they have come to trust me.

When I use the tools, I have better results if I take the

attitude that it's all an experiment or an enjoyable game. Then I enter a world of play. Giving up the fear of being wrong is easier when we're having fun.

Almost six years after I first saw the eleven blue dots connected by red lines on the tree trunk, I heard of scalar energy, about which engineer, inventor and researcher Tom Paladino has made an in depth study. As he explains it, there are two energies in the universe, electro-magnetism and scalar energy, also known by such names as chi, prana, zero point energy, and orgone. Scalar energy is responsible for the geometric form of the universe. Our sun and other stars in the Universe emit this type of energy. Scalar energy pre-exists as a connection between the stars and the Earth. It is the energy source for stellar activity, and it creates physical matter such as the stars. It also is responsible for assembling physical matter from the ether.

Put in another way, it provides the informational input, or divine instructions, responsible for the formation and the geometry of DNA in all life species. It transcends time and space. The Universe uses this Life Force to communicate with itself instantly. Scalar energy has velocities billions of times greater than the electromagnetic speed of light. When scientists discover more about how to use it, scalar energy has the potential to make space travel almost instantaneous.[1]

It has not only the ability to assemble physical mass, but it is a part of our thought processes and emotions. Every prayer, thought, emotion or physical action broadcasts scalar energy. What we broadcast comes back to us in experiences or physical properties of a similar energy vibration. That's one reason why our thoughts, emotions and actions are so powerful and why

---

[1] Tom Paladino Scalar Energy, *tompaladinoscalarenergy.com*

it's vital to learn to control them. When we raise our vibrational frequency level through such activities as meditation and prayer, we dwell on a more positive and peaceful plane.

Several prominent scientists have studied scalar energy over the last 100 plus years, among them Nikolai A. Kozyrev, Nikola Tesla, Antoine Priore, T. Galen Hieronymus, and Thomas Henry Moray. Tom Paladino studied the work of these scientists and the devices and inventions they created, and he is working to resurrect and improve upon what they developed. Using scalar energy, the scientists he studied created ways to provide relatively inexpensive and safe energy to the world. They also invented a machine that cured cancer and other diseases by reprogramming DNA to its perfect state, and they used a special device that extracted solar energy from the Universe without the benefit of power lines. The device improved radio communication so that broadcasts could penetrate directly through the Earth and be heard on the other side of the world. Some working devices of these scientists were destroyed, rejected or ignored by business or government interests due to fear of how they might be competitive or threaten national safety.

Before I heard about scalar energy, I used to discount my initial thought that what I saw on the tree trunk was a gift from the stars. I thought my initial intuitive understanding must have been mistaken. But when I read about scalar energy, I began to wonder if my original interpretation of those dots and lines on the tree might be accurate. Maybe it is a road map between stars. Maybe the stars are able to communicate with us in ways we never imagined.

CHAPTER 1

HEALING TOOLS

These healing tools are remarkable aids that represent only a sampling of the many implements available to help us heal. When I began to understand the nature of each one, I experimented with them using my imagination. As you study this category, you may find other ways to use the tools, or you may think of new ones.

The idea of using healing tools that you can't hold in your hand because they're not visible seems farfetched. Are the tools evidence of ego mania? Flights of fancy? A hint of madness? Immense gullibility? I acknowledge they could be all of those things. But I also sense an element of truth, a spark of possibility in what the tools have to offer. I choose to see them as gifts from a vast, wiser part of the Divine that knows more than I, in my human form, will ever comprehend.

Even though these tools are wonderful gifts, I never consider them the only solution to a problem. Consult your primary care physician or medical specialist about any health issue that affects you. In situations that involve poisonous bites, serious injury, life threatening illness, or any concerning symptom, immediately seek medical attention.

FIRST TOOL - POWER BOX

The first tool describes power boxes that generate energy to operate light fingers, an implement that a cottonwood named the Light Fingers Tree revealed to me. To use light fingers, let energy flow through your heart, then move down your arms into your fingers, which will glow with healing light. Your left hand receives healing energy while your right hand probes to discover needy areas. Your fingers can grow as long as needed, free of the restraints of time and space, to deliver healing energy anywhere.

The power boxes act as transformers in your hands that modulate energy flowing through your light fingers. In that way, light fingers deliver the right vibrational frequency to neutralize viruses and bacteria or to turn anything to cinders.

These power boxes are capable of operating many sets of light fingers at one time. I suspect they may draw energy from nearby land and air or from some internal source linked to the Divine. When healers tap into that energy, light fingers work flawlessly. I like to think that the power boxes symbolize the energy of God held within our hands.

SECOND TOOL - PORTAL

This tool opens a space between the seventh cranial vertebra (C-7) and the first thoracic vertebra (T-1) through which light fingers can enter and exit a person's body. This portal is one of the places where healing energy easily comes into the body. Information is absorbed with ease through this portal. When light fingers touch this part of the body, they signal the portal to open.

This point between C-7 and T-1 is an important place to treat and to protect. Those who know Reiki may use the Usui Dai-Ko-Myo symbol, learned at the Reiki Master level, to protect the portal. An energetic shield, such as the one that students receive during shamanic training, also works. Other protections could be wearing a necklace that contains a crystal such as citrine, amethyst or kyanite. Prayer and meditation also help.

When a healer's light fingers enter a body through this

portal with the intent to heal, they can probe for anything unhealthy. Energy from light fingers zaps the unhealthy material, pulverizes it and encloses it like a bag.

Once light fingers have found and collected all unhealthy material, it is time for the light fingers to leave the body through the portal and deposit the bag of cinders in a sturdy box that can withstand great heat. Imagine using a blow torch to zap anything that needs to be pulverized more. Then ask Archangel Michael to take the bag to the Light, where its contents will be transformed into something positive.

It is important never to use the portal to enter someone's body unless the person has given you permission. Healers who violate this guideline are compromising their own healing abilities and their own safety. We have angels, spirit guides and other divine helpers who assist us in the healing process, but if we continue to violate Universal laws of love, respect and individual choice, those helpers may desert us, leaving us unprotected and powerless. The negative energy we put into play by violating someone else's space will have repercussions for us. Like an overabundance of barnacles on the bottom of a boat, that negative energy will eventually incapacitate us or greatly reduce our effectiveness.

THIRD TOOL - SEED REMOVER

This tool is a technique that removes the cause of any disease from the body. Initially, the tool went by the name Leyvon Cluster. Later when there were so many tools that I couldn't remember them all, I renamed it Seed Remover to correspond with what it does. However, I call the elms that first showed me how to use the tool the Leyvon Cluster Trees.

To use the tool, imagine that you are placing one hand - it doesn't matter which hand - over the top of a person's head. If you are working with an aspect of nature such as a tree, mountain, river or bush, imagine your hand above its highest point. In that hand, see yourself holding a cluster of narrow rods made of a firm but pliant substance. They splay at the top into tiny strips that fan out, like soft fluff.

While holding this tool upright over a person's head, turn it in a counter-clockwise circle several times. When this tool was first revealed to me, a cluster of elm trees in a neighbor's yard drew my attention. I imagined holding the rods over the tops of those trees and turning my hand in a counter-clockwise circle several times. Suddenly, a ball of energy that looked like a white seed burst from the treetops. It had been imbedded somewhere in the cluster of trees, causing inflammation.

Curious about how the tool would work on people, I tried it on my husband, whose back was hurting. As I imagined moving the rods over his head several times, out popped many bean-like seeds. It happened so fast I questioned whether it really occurred. When the pain in his back decreased, it was easier for me to believe that what I saw in my mind really did happen.

FOURTH TOOL - PAIN AID

This tool, a close relative of the Seed Remover, takes inflammation, pain and scarring from the body. It looks like a red square slightly curved on the top. To use it, put it where pain, scarring or inflammation seems to originate. The tool's size can expand or contract as needed, from as small as a tooth to as large as an entire body.

To use Pain Aid, the person in pain does not have to be physically present. You can work long distance with a willing person or part of nature. After gaining their permission, imagine that you are placing the tool over the area of their discomfort. Pain, inflammation and scarring absorb into the cloth, which causes them to dissolve and disintegrate. In one session, you may need to move the tool to several different places. As one area is cleared, another spot may show up that needs attention.

FIFTH TOOL - MUCUS REMOVER

To use this tool, imagine a large stack of sticky pads that absorb well. Intend to place them inside the lungs to absorb mucus. They also work on the sinuses, intestines, and other places where mucus forms. The pads soak up not only mucus but other unwanted substances such as toxins.

If you use this tool, guide it with your heart and mind. When one pad is full, imagine removing it. Ask Mother Earth to transform it and its contents into something positive. If the area needs more attention, apply a new pad in its place. Continue the process until you sense that all the unwanted mucus has been removed. Don't worry about running out of sticky pads. The supply is as unlimited as your ability to imagine them.

SIXTH TOOL - VACUUM BRUSHES

When I first visualized this tool, it looked like a combination between a vacuum cleaner and a paint brush. It cleans out and suctions up any unwanted material in the lungs, sinuses, intestines, teeth, gums, and anywhere else in the body. It works well for cleaning around surgical sites, and it can reduce scar tissue.

Inside the paint brush is a compartment to hold what you've vacuumed up. When the compartment is full, it can be emptied into a special bag that archangels take wherever it needs to go to be transmuted into something positive. The brush can inject a substance that shrinks or loosens stuck objects. It also reduces inflammation and tension in the muscles caused by physical or emotional toxins.

SEVENTH TOOL - CUPCAKES

These tools are a series of cupcake shaped objects made from ground-up plant solids and liquids. They remind me of mud cakes. However, as with the other tools, they are non-physical, so you don't have to find mud or herbs to mix together. Simply imagine that you have all the ingredients you need even though you don't know what the ingredients are. Ask your guides and angels to direct the process as you shape the mixture into cupcakes. See yourself placing this cupcake mixture on vertebrae to ease them back into place or to dissolve bone spurs and other deposits that have grown around them.

The cupcakes also may be put on skin cancers and on insect and snake bites. They also can be used to repair wounds and reduce the size of scars. When placed on teeth, cupcakes act like tiny scrub brushes scouring away decay. They also may be placed over intestines to soften hard bowels for easier evacuation.

EIGHTH TOOL - NERVE REGENERATOR

This pepper-like material can be shaken onto nerves and cells to correct glitches in them and to regenerate them if necessary. Shake it over the top of the skin. It will find its way to the area in need of help. The nerve regenerator can recreate missing nerves or cells. In the case of injury to the skeleton, it can rebuild nerves that could lead to improved function.

It may be used in the brain to reconnect and grow synapses, enhance memory, and ease the symptoms of dementia in its many forms. In fetuses it may be used to address irregularities in nerves and cells. I have no idea what this pepper-like material is made of. I accept whatever it is as a gift from the wisdom of the Universe. Perhaps someday scientifically gifted inventors will come up with their own physical version of this tool to help the vast majority of us who can't imagine using a non-physical tool to improve our health.

NINTH TOOL - CAMERA-COMMUNICATOR

This camera, which includes a sophisticated communication system, can travel anywhere on the inside or outside of the body. It takes a picture of damaged or malformed body parts that are not likely to heal on their own. It then communicates with other body parts, assigning them tasks to fix the problem.

The tool also sends light impulses to the problem area to promote healing. These pulses send encoded messages that the cells and other parts of the body understand. They respond quickly to carry out the needed task.

The camera-communicator is vital to help all parts of the body recognize what needs to be done. If people in any of the many healing professions give the body instructions, through medication, surgery, exercise, or alternative healing techniques, the body will do its best to comply. But it can become confused if it gets more stimulation than it can handle. The camera communicator acts as an interpreter and director to help the body understand exactly what it needs to do.

TENTH TOOL - MIRROR

This tool looks a bit like a sophisticated dental mirror with a long handle. The tool is actually an intricate layer of mirrors strategically positioned to look deeply into the body.

It is placed above the top of a person's head at the crown chakra, which provides a clear connection with the divine when that chakra is working well. If this connection is foggy or closed, people can develop cerebral dysfunctions, feel spiritually bereft, experience chronic exhaustion for no apparent reason, or have extreme sensitivity to light, sound or other things in the environment.

Imagine placing the mirror above the top of the head, facing toward the sky. The mirror captures divine light, then shines it through the body, rebalancing the crown chakra. The light also stimulates targeted cells and other body parts, recalibrating them to resonate with the memory that they are perfectly formed and free of any dysfunction.

CHAPTER 2

WARRIOR TOOLS

These tools are not ones I would have associated with warriors. When I revealed the first few to my friend who worked with the energy of water, he was skeptical. For him, warrior tools went hand in hand with force. They must overpower or destroy the enemy. They must dominate others so they will obey. They must exert control and demand obedience.

However, these warrior tools address a truth about real power that goes beyond force. They show us how to align ourselves with divine purpose so we can strengthen our connection with God. Our greatest strength lies in that connection, which is forged not by weapons of war but by remembering the powerful, innocent, loving, changeless beings we are, created in God's image to spend eternity with him.

FIRST TOOL - SPIRIT OF SACRIFICE

When the trees taught me about this tool, they tied it to an experience that was happening in my life at that moment. This method of teaching helps me to better grasp the essence of the tool. In this case, the event was the death of my 14-year-old cat, Molly, named because of her motley color. She wasn't pretty to look at, but she had the sweetest disposition.

When my best friend came to visit one day, she picked Molly up, held her and petted her for several minutes. Though Molly seemed fine, my friend sensed water pouring from her and a capsule breaking open in her body. At first she thought the capsule might represent a tumor that we didn't know the cat had. After Molly died sometime that night, my friend realized the water was an image of Molly's spirit making the decision to leave her body. When the capsule opened, it showed the moment when Molly's spirit began to separate from her body.

I buried Molly by the irrigation ditch bridge so I could pass her grave every time I visited the trees and the river. As soon as I finished burying her, her spirit floated out of the ground. She grew gigantic! She stood on the bridge beside Schutzengel, an angel that protects our property. My heart filled with gratitude when I understood the magnificent gift Molly had given to Schutzengel and me. She recognized the angel needed help, and she gave up her physical life so that in her more powerful, non-physical state, she could help Schutzengel protect the land and the people in it, including me. Through that spirit of sacrifice she fulfilled her purpose in a much bigger way than she ever could have as my pet cat. She understood that her body was only a temporary house and that her spirit no longer needed it.

As I mulled over the spirit of sacrifice tool, it seemed to mean more than passing from this life to fulfill a greater purpose. It involves nurturing a connection with divinity so that we understand when it's time for us to move in a different direction. When we keep that link with God strong, it's easier for us to recognize which fork in the road to take next, which pathway will help us fulfill our higher purpose.

Sometimes the next pathway involves a true desire to help another person. It means setting aside our own goals and purposes for a few moments to focus on another's need. We sacrifice our own desires to provide that help, whether it's performing a physical task or spending time in prayer and meditation to focus on someone's non-physical needs.

Kabbalah scholar Michael Berg said it well in his book, *What God Meant*. "Even if we are evil," he wrote, "even if we have no Light, no special claim to virtue, as long as we truly have a desire to help another person, that desire will connect us to the Creator and will give us all the strength and Light that we need to provide that help. ... If we have a true desire to help the other person - even if we are not worthy, even if we are not right - we can still be the conduit to help another." [2]

That path of sacrificing our own needs long enough to help another is paved with love, kindness, and support. God, whose nature is unconditional love, will not ask us to take a pathway that leads to violence. If you feel drawn to do something that will physically or emotionally harm yourself or others, you're not using the spirit of sacrifice tool. You're being influenced by someone or something that does not have your best interests or your highest purpose at heart. Instead, center yourself in God's unconditional love. Feel grounded in that love and let it completely surround you. In the light of that love, rethink whatever you've contemplated doing. If you need help, seek the counsel of someone wise and loving whom you trust.

This tool reminds us that sometimes it's wise to let go of goals, ideas, work or personal relationships that are no longer healthy for us even though that may, at first, seem like sacrifices that we don't want to make. Letting go can be scary. It often feels safer to hang onto a familiar but unhappy or dead-end situation than to step into the uncertainty of newer and brighter possibilities.

As kids, we used to play a game on the third story balcony of our school. The open air porch had a sturdy wooden

---

[2] Berg, Michael, *What God Meant*, Kabbalah Publishing, Los Angeles, CA, 2009, pp. 28-29.

enclosure all around it. We would stand a few feet away from the railings, close our eyes, and walk slowly toward the edge of the porch as though nothing was there to keep us from falling. The heady thrill of danger made our hearts beat faster. When we reached the railing, we gripped its solid support, thankful we could count on its protection.

When we choose to sacrifice what's safe and reliable and step into a new experience that will help us grow and move us toward our next goal, it can feel scary. It's like walking toward the end of the balcony. It's helpful to remember that we're surrounded by angels, spirit guides and other divine helpers who are all rooting for us to succeed. If we trust that a solid railing of protection surrounds us, the spirit of sacrifice can feel more like the spirit of adventure.

SECOND TOOL - LOVE

When it came time for me to know the second tool, I asked my friend who conversed naturally with trees to identify it. As we stood by the Twinkling Lights Tree, she saw in her mind a temple or sacred shrine, something that provided protection and whose essence was love, an incredibly powerful force. And so the second tool's name became Love.

We wear love like a protection with the knowledge that love is stronger than anything. It both nurtures and protects us, and it provides a wide array of divine help from both the seen and unseen realms when circumstances call for decisive action.

If you feel drained of energy when you are around someone, broadcast love from yourself to the environment around you, and include the person you find it hard to be around. The act of sending out love will help your energy remain strong. When love flows out from you, it protects you and keeps your energy from being drained. [3]

Children who grow up in difficult, sometimes unsafe circumstances often become resilient if they have just one person in their life who offers them nurturing love and support. This tool is all about that love. It equips us with a knowing that we have someone in our corner. If someone cares enough to go to bat for us, that can make all the difference. We may become that tool for others, offering caring support so they know they're not alone.

THIRD TOOL - ARROW

Unlike an arrow meant to wound or kill someone, this arrow aligns our intent with the will of God. When we ask God to guide us, he will direct us as straight and sure as an arrow.

Through the intent to align with God's will, we join all who seek to follow the Divine plan for their lives. In that way, we become whole, united in a common purpose.

The arrow tool can be found on each side of a triangle. One of those sides connects us with people and other living things. Another side grounds us to Mother Earth, and the third side unites is with God. As you imagine the triangle, identify what role each side plays. Though each side is not really an arrow, think of each line as though it were an arrow with a point at both ends of the line. In that way, the arrow points in both directions, and its nurturing energy flows both ways.

---

[3] Roman, Sanaya, *Personal Power through Awareness*, HJ Kramer Inc., Tiburon, California, 1986, p. 22

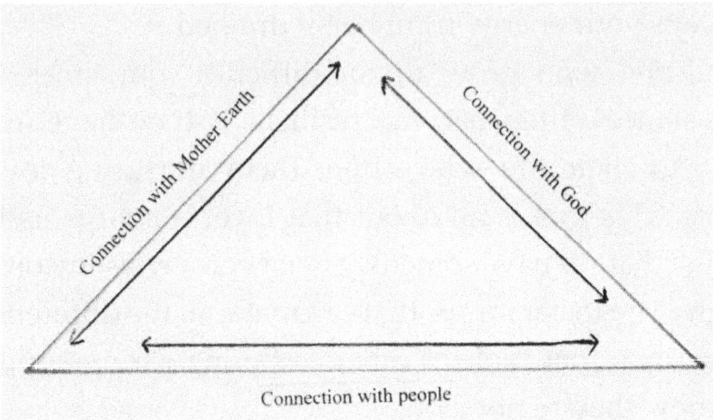

If you feel weak, unsure, scatterbrained, or out of sorts, close your eyes and imagine seeing each line that forms the triangle. Imagine that triangle superimposed over you. Is one line crooked or broken? Notice which side of the triangle that line is on. It will give you an idea of where your weakness lies - in your connection with Mother Earth, with God or with other people.

Take time to focus your thoughts on each of those lines. Watch how they realign and become straighter and unbroken. Feel the strength that comes from a perfectly formed triangle.

When these lines are balanced, straight and unbroken, you will have the strength of a mighty warrior. You can focus on whatever problem you face and receive the help you need.

FOURTH TOOL - LIGHT OF GOD'S PRESENCE

When we focus the light of God's presence on anything, whatever is not of God disappears. The light engulfs it and dissolves it. It may help to think of the light of God's presence as the most powerful weapon, because nothing can withstand it. Anything that comes in contact with it dissolves into it as it is transformed and becomes part of that light. It is a potent, mighty tool.

It can be difficult to use this tool, because the challenges and circumstances we face sometimes make us feel so overwhelmed that we forget about the light. The best way I've found to use this tool is to spend time in prayer and meditation, seeking guidance. Then do everything you can to handle the situation while trusting that unseen help, working on your behalf in the background, will resolve the problem. Be open to ideas that sprout in your mind. You may discover that your problems are handled in remarkable ways you never imagined possible. But first you must do all you can to move things forward. An experience in Arizona many years ago helped me to understand that concept.

Upon graduating from college in the late 1960s, I took a job for a year at a Bureau of Indian Affairs dormitory in Arizona. After that first year, I found a job as a public school teacher in Arizona. But I didn't have all the teaching credentials I needed for a permanent teaching certificate. Getting a one-year waiver meant traveling to Phoenix to fill out paperwork. I didn't know if I stood a chance of receiving that waiver. If I couldn't get it, I wouldn't have enough time to meet state requirements that would qualify me for a permanent certificate by the next school year. That meant I would be out of a job.

After spending a lot of time in prayer, I drove the few hundred miles to the state capital, found the correct office, and filled out the necessary paperwork. I was told I could go home and be notified by mail or wait in case a decision was made that day. I chose to wait.

For two long hours I sat on a wooden bench in that office. Worried thoughts swirled through my mind. Would I get the waiver? Would I be forced to quit my job? Would I have to move back home and live with my parents? Finally, I closed my eyes and prayed. Peace settled around me. The room seemed to fill with light.

A door opened, and a man approached with a paper in his hand. It was my waiver! I had done everything I could to get it, and I'd left the rest up to God. The Light of God's Presence tool can work behind the scenes on your behalf just as it did for me.

FIFTH TOOL - POWER OF WORSHIP

Where two or three of us are gathered in God's name, we unite the divine spark that is in each of us. With that greater light, we catch a glimpse of our Oneness and our limitless abundance. Worship connects us with the knowledge that we carry within each of us a piece of God. When those pieces come together in worship, they shed a bigger light. Unconditional love and support that comes from worship can provide soothing, healing, and amazing results.

While in college, a group of us decided to gather early one Easter morning for our own Easter sunrise service under trees that marked the edges of fields around the campus. After spending a few moments in worship together, we each found a quiet, private place to commune with God alone. Birds chirped, rabbits scuttled through the underbrush, and a mild breeze rustled tree branches. During that quiet time, each of us received an insight or a verse of scripture answering concerns that weighed on our minds. We came back together, sharing the wisdom we'd found, and our faith and enthusiasm for life grew stronger. I found a scripture that reminded me I am never alone, never without the help I need, always surrounded by God's love no matter what the situation. That reminder sustained me for many months.

Use the worship tool frequently. It will help you catch a greater glimpse of how powerful and wise you are and how limitless is the supply of help that surrounds you.

SIXTH TOOL - WEATHER CONTROL

When mastered, this tool provides the power to control nature and all the elements. It lets you manifest snow by sensing that it already surrounds you. Use your imagination to create the sense that you are already standing in the snow. Hear it crunch under your boots, see it blanket the ground and drape pine boughs. Imagine running your hands through it as you shape it into snowballs. Feel its coldness on your skin. Taste its earthiness as it melts on your tongue.

Use all your senses to imagine that you are already standing in whatever element you want to manifest. Savor the pleasure of imagining it into being. Feel the happy abandon of mud squishing through your toes in the rain. Let excitement fill you as wind billows boat sails. Bask in the protection of fog nestled close to the ground. Whatever kind of weather you want to create, determine what that weather is, imagine you are experiencing it right now, and enjoy the pleasure of being surrounded by it.

If you want to control the weather, don't wish for a certain kind of weather or want it to occur. In that frame of mind, you are stating that you don't yet have it, you're simply wishing for it or wanting it. Instead, imagine experiencing it in the moment as though it's already happening.

When I was studying for my Ph.D. in metaphysics, I wrote my doctoral dissertation on a special kind of prayer. This form of prayer is outlined in the Essene Gospel of Peace, part of the Dead Sea Scrolls. Gregg Braden, a best-selling author who has bridged science and ancient wisdom, explained how to use that prayer method in his cassette tape series, *"Speaking the Lost*

Language of God." [4]

This special kind of prayer is one way to manifest whatever you want, including a certain kind of weather. It works by creating within yourself an emotion of love. This could be love of life, love of someone near and dear to you or love of something such as peace, harmony, or the elaborate tree house you built for your children. The emotion of love can be hard to muster if you've been going through tough times. In that case, focus on a tiny ray of hope, determination, courage, fondness, gratitude or another positive emotion.

After you have stirred up that emotion in yourself, concentrate on a thought that describes what you want. My dissertation involved a project I called Peace in Farmington, NM, which is the largest city near where I live. When I focused on what I wanted to create, my thought was "Peace in Farmington," not "I want peace in Farmington" or "I wish there was peace in Farmington," but the present tense right now reality of being surrounded by peace in Farmington.

I let the emotion of love and the thought of peace in Farmington combine to create the feeling that peace encompassed me. Each time I prayed with an emotion of love or something close to it, various feelings resulted. Sometimes I felt a sense of security, safety or joy. At other times I felt contentment or harmony. For as long as you have the time or desire to pray, repeat the thought of what you want and allow yourself to feel that it is a reality right now. In my case, I simply repeated the phrase, "Peace in Farmington" and felt it surrounding me.

People who agreed to be part of the project also prayed the

---

[4] Braden, Gregg, *Speaking the Lost Language of God*, Nightingale Conant, 6245 West Howard

prayer, "Peace in Farmington," and together we had a positive impact on the city. Though the results were not large enough to be statistically significant, they showed drops in crimes, fires and visits to the emergency room during the month covered by the prayer experiment. The police officer who gathered statistics for me was also the officer called to the most violent crimes. He said he had fewer than normal calls to violent crimes that month.

Though weather control and increasing peace are two very different goals, the Essene prayer can be effective for just about anything. Experiment with controlling weather by using the prayer. Play with it and see what kind of results you get.

Some people have learned to speak to the consciousness of wind and other elements of nature to bring about a change in the weather. One of them is Helena Messenger, a clairvoyant healer who developed Morphogenic Field Therapy to diagnose the cause of people's treatment issues. Once the issue is diagnosed, she clears, balances, and integrates each person's mental, emotional, spiritual and physical bodies. She can speak to anything that has consciousness, from parasites and ghosts to wind and water.

Several years ago when a fire threatened a town in northwest Colorado, she helped to lessen property damage caused by that fire. In his book *Adventures with Master Leeney, Book One: Shackle's Key*, her friend, Gary Robertson, wrote about how her intervention worked.

"When I heard about the fire," he quoted her as saying, "I talked to the wind devas and asked them what this was all about. They said they needed the fire to cleanse some negative energy created by several groups of people working with dark magic, something like satanic ritual. I asked the devas if they needed to burn the whole town. They said no, but questioned, why not? It wasn't a big deal to them. Because a lot of people would suffer needlessly, I told them, 'Can't you burn the area you need cleansed and leave the town alone?' They talked it over among themselves and agreed, yes, they could do that. So they shifted the wind and burned only the area on the west side of town where the dark energy was." [5]

Though this is not a talent that everyone shares, if you want to cultivate it, first call on your angels and other spirit helpers who operate in the light of unconditional love, asking them to protect and assist you. Then speak to the consciousness of wind, rain or other elements of nature in an effort to connect with them. Listen to what they have to say. You contain a spark of God within you, and so do they, so treat them with respect. If you keep practicing, you may discover you are one of those gifted people who can communicate with nature and negotiate a positive change.

SEVENTH TOOL - STAYING GROUNDED

This tool is more powerful than many people realize. Not only does it keep you connected to the Earth and to God, but it keeps your power center, located in your abdominal area near your navel, strong no matter what challenges you may face.

There are many ways to ground yourself. Find one that works well for you and use it several times a week. Here are a few suggestions.

1. Imagine you are lying on a soft green lawn. Feel the firmness of the Earth under you.
2. Savor the sun's rays warming your face. Sense that the Earth's firmness and the sun's warmth are

---

[5] Robertson, Gary, *Adventures with Master Leeney, Book One: Shackle's Key*, Springs Foundation, 2007, pp. 164-165

weaving a powerful cord connecting you to Earth and sky.

3. Notice energy flowing from high above you, moving on a line through the center of your body and going deep into the Earth. From the Earth, two lines rise, passing outside both sides of your feet and legs at an angle. Those lines stop somewhere outside your heart level. Two other lines angle down from above your head and connect with the lines rising from the Earth. They form a diamond shape around your body. On the back side of your body a similar diamond shape forms.

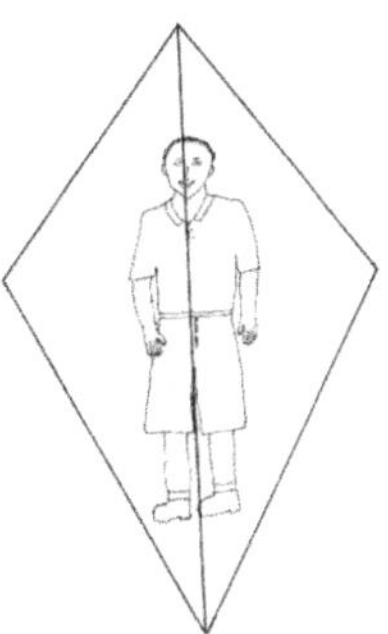

The front and back edges of those diamonds meet, enfolding you in a protective shield. As that double diamond shape creates a shield around you, it also descends deep into the Earth and rises into the sky, helping you to ground firmly with both Earth and with God. Imagine being enfolded by that diamond. Feel the power of its protection, and be aware of the strength you feel when you're inside the double diamond.

4. Sense that a white or golden light above you flows through the top of your head, down through your body and out through your feet into the ground.

Then feel the nourishing, nurturing essence of Mother Earth travel up through your feet, into your body and out the top of your head, connecting you once again with God. Sometimes the flow of energy from Mother Earth may take on different colors. It may have the color of rich, black, nutritious soil. At other times it might carry pastel shades, different hues or no color at all. Acknowledge and appreciate whatever you see. To enhance the grounded feeling, imagine that the light of God's presence is flowing through the top of your head and settling in your power center, slightly below your belly button. Then imagine the rich nurturing energy of Mother Earth moving up through your feet and legs until it reaches your power center, where it joins the light of God's presence, creating a firm, powerful anchor.

5. In a variation of number 4, imagine two golden threads are traveling from the bottoms of your feet deep into the core of Mother Earth. Imagine shooting those golden cords down to the center of the Earth. If you have trouble moving them downward, let Mother Earth pull them down to her core. Next, imagine a silver thread traveling from the top of your head all the way up to the sun. When you feel that strong thread anchor into the sun, breathe in the sun's light. Let it travel down the silver cord, through your body, and descend on the golden cords attached to the bottom of your feet. Let the light flow all the way down those golden cords to the Earth's core. Repeat that breath several times. As you breathe the light from the sun through your body into the Earth's core, let it take from you any

physical or emotional pain. Mother Earth can easily transmute this pain into something positive. She wants to do this for you and has been waiting for you to ask for her help.

6. Imagine that a huge tuning fork surrounds you with its top pointing to the sky and its two prongs delving deep into the ground. Feel God's presence flow through the top of that tuning fork at your head. Follow it down around your body until it anchors into the ground, completely surrounding you with vibrating, powerful, rejuvenating energy.
7. Starting with your head, become aware of every part of your body, from your eyes, nose, mouth and throat to your shoulders, arms, torso, legs and feet. Feel every part of your body pulse with energy. Notice how connected everything feels. Sense your firm connection to the Earth.

Experiment with different grounding methods. Ask your divine helpers to assist you in finding a technique that works well for you. As you practice it, you may feel that you are less susceptible to taking on other people's emotions and not as likely to carry their burdens. Instead, your energy will remain high enough that you are no longer drained by other people's energy or by whatever is going on around you.

EIGHTH TOOL - PRAISE

The act of praise strengthens your connection with God and keeps your own energy level high. Praise God and all divine helpers who assist you. Express thanks for all they do. As you surround yourself with the power of praise and the light of its positive energy, negativity fades. You see more clearly how to handle difficult and challenging situations and people.

If you sense you've been fighting a battle with impossible odds, expect an "aha" moment, a burst of inspiration, when you step into an attitude of praise. You will catch a glimmer of how to approach challenges differently to gain better results.

I experienced how powerful praise can be when a friend, who'd moved away after a divorce, phoned to tell me she'd lost her two children in a court battle with her ex-husband. I could hear the pain in her voice as she asked, "Will you come?" I promised I'd drive to where she was staying in a motel 15 miles away as soon as my husband returned with the car.

I paced the floor as I waited. What could I do to help her? What if I said the wrong thing? Why didn't my husband hurry home? I didn't think I was smart enough, wise enough, well trained enough to help my friend in her hour of need. Fear needled my thoughts and tied me up in knots of perceived helplessness.

In desperation, I dialed a friend to seek advice. The phone wouldn't ring. I dialed again. Still no ring. When I phoned my husband to ask him to hurry home, I couldn't reach him. I was alone, stuck at home with no way to reach my needy friend. The more agitated and frustrated I felt, the harder it was for me to connect with guidance available from divine wisdom.

When there was nowhere else to turn, I finally asked God for help. First, I thanked him for the opportunity to help my friend and for the trust she had placed in me. My mind began to clear a little, though it still felt sluggish with worry, concern and fear. Gradually, as I continued to pray, calmness settled over me. I thanked God for that calmness. As I continued in an attitude of praise, my mind cleared even more.

Different synonyms for the word "rejected" flooded my brain, so many I couldn't remember them all. But I didn't have to. Just one of those words helped me to understand how my friend was feeling. With that knowledge, I could pray for her better and have the confidence to speak the right words when we met face to face.

My husband soon returned with the car, and I drove to my friend's motel room. She was so glad to see me! Just my presence, not anything I said or did, made a difference to her. Though I couldn't solve her problems, I could show her what a valued person she was in my life and that I accepted her no matter what problems she faced. As we spent time together, I thanked God for calming my mind enough that I could help my friend.

Praise connects us with divine wisdom. It's a powerful tool. It's part of scalar energy that connects everyone and everything in the universe together.

NINTH TOOL - TIME TRAVEL

At first, this tool seemed impossible to me. Can anyone really time travel? Isn't it in the realm of fantasy? When I asked my divine helpers to show me this tool in a way I could understand, I saw light impulses. Those impulses, which represent vibrational frequencies, allow our souls to instantly travel anyplace inside or outside the bounds of time. We are not limited by space or time. We are one with everything, and we instantly travel from within to everywhere. Though I didn't realize it then, I was seeing an example of scalar energy at work.

Instead of time travel, we are really using timeless travel or outside-of-time travel. Using this tool, we can visit other planets, realms, or universes and meet beings who can teach us new skills, such as how to perform a task, develop a talent, or handle a challenging situation. Everything we could possibly need is available to us in this way.

I glimpsed how that works when the Portal Tree showed me that everything and everywhere is already within me. It's part of me as I am part of it. All time, all space, all stars, planets, universes are within me. I go within to everywhere. Tuning into that reality makes it possible to travel anywhere, even to the farthest stars, in the blink of an eye. They're already part of us, and we're part of them. We are part of All that Is. We are part of divinity. We are One with the Source of all things. So it makes sense that we're interconnected. This is an extraordinary way to view the Universe and beyond.

If you use your mind to try and figure out this tool, it will most likely elude you. The few times I've scratched the surface of understanding it have been when I came from a heartfelt attitude of trust and didn't try to understand how it worked. I leave that to scientific geniuses who are able to think in ways I can't begin to comprehend with my mind, but sometimes I grasp them on a different level with my heart. That's when gratitude swells the boundaries of my heart, and I experience for a moment the reality of our Oneness with divinity. In that state of awareness, time travel seems possible.

TENTH TOOL - BLEND INTO THE BACKGROUND

This tool requires that we give up the need to be recognized for our accomplishments. It involves blending in so well that people don't notice us. In this way, we are able to work in the background without being spotted and do important things that can make the difference between success and failure for ourselves and others. It lets us do what needs to be done without experiencing opposition.

When circumstances require it, people don't notice us and, in essence, we become invisible. One way to practice this skill is to sit on a bench in a large store. Keep your eyes open but don't make eye contact with anyone. See if you can blend into the background so well that no one will notice you even if they sit on the same bench.

When you get good enough at using this tool, people won't pay attention to what you're doing. You can provide whatever assistance is needed in challenging places or circumstances without being spotted. People don't stop you from helping to make the world a better place.

If you can't become invisible because of your desire to be recognized for an accomplishment, don't get upset with yourself. Sometimes that recognition is necessary and important. Practice invisibility when it's easy to give up being recognized for something you've done. When you get good at practicing invisibility with little things, it will be easier to practice invisibility in other circumstances as well.

CHAPTER 3

COMMUNICATION TOOLS

Good communication is the key to success in any venture. We communicate in subtle ways through body language and in more sophisticated ways through technological advances as well as through writing, speaking and acting.

Some tools the Power Tree revealed to me seem so simple that I wondered if I had misunderstood. How could taste, touch and smell be communication tools? We take our senses for granted, but they play important roles. They hone our concentration, sharpen our senses, make us more aware of what's happening around us.

Being a good communicator means paying attention to subtle signals in our immediate surroundings. Magicians who claim to be mind readers perform their tricks by keenly observing every eye movement, muscle twitch, swallow and toss of the hand or head. Those clues tell them what a person is thinking. People can tell if someone is lying by using those same techniques. Tuning into your five senses helps you stay more alert so you can be a better communicator and a better interpreter of what others are thinking.

In spite of the leaps we have made in this field, we've only scratched the surface of the potential that communication holds in our Universe and beyond. These ten tools provide a glimmer of the possibilities and far flung opportunities that still await our comprehension.

FIRST TOOL - STAR CONNECTION

This tool reminds me of a sophisticated tower that makes it

possible for communication to occur between people on Earth and in far off parts of the Universe. Astrologists tell us that stars have an effect on our emotions and on the ease with which we can accomplish things during certain times. So we know stars have some kind of influence. Heavenly bodies much closer to us, such as the moon, are known to affect us as well. For example, law enforcement officers have noticed that crimes increase when there's a full moon.

In the last half of the 20th century, scientists scanned the skies and listened for non-random patterns of electromagnetic emissions from outer space in a program called SETI: The Search for Extraterrestrial Intelligence. They wanted to find out if we are all alone in this vast universe and beyond or if other intelligent life exists. These listening devices required sophisticated scientific equipment.

However, the star connection tool requires no equipment at all. Unlike advanced hardware, this tool is related to an awareness that we are all part of the whole, we are all One, like a hologram. If one tiny piece of a hologram is cut away, that sliver still contains the entire hologram. This awareness helps us to understand that we truly are all One. We are all connected with everything in the Universe and with whatever intelligent life may be out there.

To use this tool, meditate on the awareness of being connected to everything that exists. During quiet contemplation, when your mind is not too busy with everyday details, immerse yourself in this awareness. It will help you connect to the divinity in every aspect of the Universe and beyond. It will help you recognize the value in every living being.

While you practice using this tool, surround yourself with a protective shield and with the intent to interact only with energies that operate in unconditional love. Then connect with the limitless part of yourself. My friend who worked with the energy of water challenged me to go the stars one evening as we stood in my driveway looking into the night sky. No one had ever asked me such a thing before, but I discovered it was easy. I imagined I was there, and suddenly I found myself walking on the rocky surface of someplace I didn't think I'd ever been before. Without understanding how I knew this, I knew I was walking on the surface of a star. The sensation lasted only a few minutes, and then I was back in my driveway.

"How do you feel?" asked my friend.

"Homesick," I replied. I missed that star already, though I didn't understand why. Later it occurred to me that I had just visited a part of the vast Universe that seemed way out there in the vast reaches of space, but also dwells in me. It was a part of myself that I seldom noticed and had not connected with for a very long time. We travel inward to reach everywhere. If we don't do it, we miss the joy and delight of rubbing shoulders with the rest of who we are, with the vastness inside of us that we often neglect to experience.

When you use this tool, you are really learning to communicate better with yourself. In these moments, you may find answers, formulas, concepts that you never would have dreamed possible.

SECOND TOOL - UNIVERSITIES OF KNOWLEDGE

When tools first come into my mind, they sometimes arrive with a picture to help me grasp how they work. The visual aid that came with this tool was a star on which stood many buildings of different sizes and shapes. Each structure represented a university that specialized in a certain type of knowledge. When anyone requested knowledge about a subject, the responsible person in the appropriate building sent out light impulses of information to the asker.

When people with a strong desire to understand something use this tool, they hook into knowledge within the vastness of our Universe and beyond. Often people receive this information after they've spent much time trying to find solutions to a specific problem through study, introspection, or prayer. Sometimes the answer comes when they take a nap. While still asleep they may reach for a notebook on which to write the answer, which they will discover later when they awaken. Or the answer may pop into their head at odd moments. As with the Star Connection tool, the Universities of Knowledge tool works when we take time to go inward in a state of meditation, contemplation, or even sleep. In those relaxed states, it's much easier for us to access the knowledge or insight to reach a goal, perform a task, or invent something.

I experienced how well this tool works when I struggled to write descriptions for these communication tools. How could I describe them so people could grasp how important and helpful they really are? I thought about this problem often, sometimes during the day, sometimes in the evening shortly before I went to sleep.

After I awoke one morning I felt overwhelmed with the task. It was just too hard. So instead of getting out of bed, I began to read a novel. There wasn't much point in doing anything else. I had no idea how to proceed with the daunting task. When I finally climbed out of bed and my feet hit the floor, answers flooded my mind as to how to explain each tool.

Ideas sprang up, understanding blossomed, memories rekindled. The work that had once seemed overwhelming suddenly flowed with ease. I had somehow tapped into the

Universities of Knowledge tool and discovered how amazingly well it works.

THIRD TOOL - SOUND IMPULSES

As I tried to comprehend this tool, what came to mind was an image of drums made from specialized material that has not yet been developed on our planet. The drums capture sound and send it in waves everywhere. Those waves contain information for anyone who will listen. When the sound waves reach receptive ears and minds, they download as a series of clicks or vibrations, which translate into thoughts or music. People who aren't interested may hear annoying clicks, strange oscillations or nothing at all.

At times I have heard oscillating waves of energy moving inside my ears. The first time I noticed it, the waves were unnerving until I decided to relax into the experience and curiously watch what happened. After about 30 seconds, the waves settled down, then stopped. During those times, I've never been struck with a brilliant idea nor have I heard beautiful music. But I suspect that some part of my being is taking it all in and storing it away for the right moment.

Listening to those oscillating waves helps me tune everything else out. Instead of thinking about the past or worrying about the future, I am focused on the present moment. Those sound impulses keep me in the now where no judgment, doubt, anger, guilt or worry exist. The present moment is healing, calming and relaxing. In that nonjudgmental slice of time I am more receptive to hearing messages that help me find peace and wholeness.

I experienced the power of sound after my father died. I traveled to another state for his funeral. After the service, I sat on the sofa in my mother's living room, completely exhausted.

In a semi-dazed state, I heard my father's voice echoing in my head in a foreign language I'd learned as a child. He spoke two words: "Drink water." I knew it was my dad. I recognized the inflection of his voice. If I had heard those words in English, they wouldn't have carried the same impact. I went to the kitchen to get a glass of water. That hydration gave me the energy I needed to make it through the next few hours.

Some forms of meditation involve making certain sounds that can have calming, healing, or balancing effects. Two common sounds to make are "Ah" and "Om." Others include the vowel sounds, which can have an effect on certain organs.

The Sound Impulses tool has much to offer if we tune into it.

FOURTH TOOL - SMELL

Certain smells may trigger delightful or disagreeable memories. They can warn us of danger and make us feel hunger or pleasure. This particular tool spurs us to take action or to change our attitudes.

When we smell something that doesn't seem to be part of our normal daily experience, it is wise to pay attention. It may be God's way of communicating something important with us. If we smell something rotten, our frame of mind may stink. If we don't change our attitude, we could find ourselves wading in a garbage heap of problems. We may be so stuck or sluggish in our ways that we're like stagnant water. The longer it stays in one place, the more it begins to smell. Something we're doing or thinking may be so unwise, unfair, or harmful that it starts to reek.

An unpleasant smell could warn us that someone is attacking us, either to our face or behind our back. It might let us know we are holding onto false beliefs, old thought patterns that no longer serve us, or that we are letting other people's attitudes influence us.

Though we may not be aware of these subtle smells that rise from the nonphysical realm, being aware of this tool can help us to discern them. When we refer to an unpleasant situation or frame of mind by saying, "That stinks!" we're tuning into this unseen tool that warns us of trouble or of the need to change our thoughts. The smell tool helps us tune in to that deeper and wiser part of ourselves or to messages from our angels or spirit guides, warning us to be alert.

On another level, when we focus on the sense of smell, we are propelling ourselves into the present moment in the same way that the sound impulses tool does. As we hone our attention to that smell, we let go of everything else. We no longer think about the past or the future. We are so totally aware of the smell that every other thought and sensation fades and provides us a rest from all those other thoughts that have been churning through our minds. Let the tool of smell lead you to a restful place filled with greater wisdom and peacefulness.

FIFTH TOOL - TASTE

This tool has nothing to do with our normal sense of taste. What we taste when we eat food or drink liquids provides us with clues about what we've ingested. This tool, on the other hand, is a way of calling us to pay closer attention to our thoughts and motivations.

If the taste is foul, we may have been thinking about doing or saying something unkind. If the taste is metallic, we might have been harboring poisonous thoughts. Should we taste something sickeningly sweet, we may have been trying to sugar coat the truth.

On occasion, it reflects something we're trying to learn. Once when I sent distance Reiki to someone and tuned in to what that person needed, I took a drink of water. It tasted like blood. Thinking the entire container of filtered water was contaminated, I threw it out, poured in new water, and let it filter through the purification system. When I took a sip of the newly filtered water, it still tasted like blood. I finally decided it might be a message that the person needed to have a blood test. When a doctor performed the test, it uncovered minor concerns that were easy to treat before they became bigger concerns.

The taste will be different for everyone depending on the situation. As in all the communication tools, it's a method our Higher Self uses to get our attention. The better we get at interpreting the meaning behind the taste, the more useful this tool will become.

The tool of taste, just as the tools of sound and smell, can lead us into the present moment. In that space, we let go of the past and the future. We dwell in the now where we are more aware and more tuned in to the divine presence that is always available to guide us when we pay attention.

SIXTH TOOL - ELECTRICAL IMPULSES

Electrical impulses sent out by this tool act as a wake-up call to whatever part of our body needs it. Perhaps a leg or arm will twitch, a spot on your shoulder will vibrate, or an eye will pulse. Twitches, vibrations and pulses don't always mean that the tool is trying to get your attention, but the more you become aware of the tool, the better you will get at recognizing when it's trying to tell you something.

If you sense any of these responses, take a few seconds to focus on the area of your body that's affected. Then go within and meditate. Is there a message for you? Ask your angels and guides to help you understand the truth about what's happening and if important information is available to you.

These impulses may stimulate the body when it needs extra nutrition, water, or energy. Dehydration can make you feel tired, weak, stressed. The tool may send you a reminder to give your body healthy fuel so it can carry out its purpose.

One late winter day, I hiked up a long, flat hill that stretched for perhaps a quarter of a mile. The flat top made a great place for large microwave and other communication towers. Several of them were clustered in one area on the hill. The closer I got to them, the more uncomfortable I became. I felt bombarded by unpleasant energy. The electromagnetic waves traveling from those towers created havoc in my body. Because there was no other way around the towers, I moved past them as fast as I could. Those electrical impulses sent a clear message not to linger in that area.

When you start to feel that something isn't right about a location, a set of circumstances or a person, it's important to value your hunches. The electrical impulses tool may be at work, and that means it's time to pay attention.

Sometimes your Higher Self will use this tool to help you perk up and take notice. The more you become aware of how your body feels and reacts to what and who you are around, the more sensitive you will become to the guidance. The wiser, eternal part of yourself is always finding ways to help you stay focused on the purpose for which you came into this life.

SEVENTH TOOL - DOCUMENTARIES

This tool delivers detailed information about a particular subject. The knowledge can come to you in many ways. It might come through a documentary you see in a movie theater, on a DVD or on television. It could come through a book, an article, on the Internet, in a conversation or through a piece of art.

Once when I was visiting my elderly mother, I packed her wheelchair in the trunk of my car, settled her in the passenger seat, and took her on a ride downtown. She loved books, and she found great pleasure in reading children's stories to her grandkids. So I took her to the children's section of a large bookstore. While she checked out the books there, I felt drawn to a nearby section. A paperback caught my eye. It was *The Disappearance of the Universe* by Gary R. Renard. When I'd first heard about this book, I'd wanted to read it, but work and other responsibilities intervened, and I forgot about it. There it was, inviting me to take it from the shelf. I leafed through it and knew I had to have it.

When Mom was ready to go, I purchased the book. Once I started reading it, I couldn't put it down. It had so much information for which I'd been hungering. The documentary tool was at work when my mother and I visited that store.

EIGHTH TOOL - TREE PHONE

I call this tool the tree phone because it helps us to communicate more effectively with trees. The history linking trees and people is full of ups and downs. At times humans and trees have been wonderful friends who worked together to insure the health of the planet. At other times, people have been quite dismissive of trees. They have forgotten about them or deliberately mistreated or destroyed them. In their neglect, they have pushed aside the healing power that trees want to provide. As a result, our health has suffered. Oxygen levels on Earth have decreased, and plants that could heal certain diseases have become extinct.

This tool's purpose is to encourage greater respect and appreciation between trees and people. Many of us don't think about communicating with trees. We enjoy the shade they offer, the erosion control they provide, the animals that live, play and chatter in their branches, but we often don't think of trees as individual creations of God with their own personalities and gifts.

The next time you notice a tree, acknowledge it. Thank it for all it has to offer. Trees want to be acknowledged. They want to help us, and sometimes they need us to help them. This kind of communication will not occur until trees know they can trust us. That trust builds as we spend time with them, acknowledging them, praying for them, and sending them positive energy. They have an intrinsic fear of being cut down. They don't know they can trust us to treat them well unless we take the time to acknowledge and appreciate them.

When I am away from home, I like to notice the trees around me, to tell them how much I enjoy them, and to thank God for them. Sometimes a burst of joy will come from a tree. At other times, they will express a longing for communication, or they will ask for help, most often in the form of prayer. Some trees are reluctant to connect with me at first. Their trust in people isn't strong. They don't open up to me until they see other trees connect with me, then they recognize that it's safe to make contact and that it can have a positive effect on them. If one tree in an area discovers it can trust me, more reluctant trees soon follow suit. As that trust grows, it gets passed from tree to tree and from place to place. Now when I'm away from home, trees I've never seen before reach out to connect with me. They sometimes give me messages for trees back home.

Trees have a communication system of their own that stretches around the world. When word spreads that certain people respect, appreciate, and acknowledge trees, trees respond in kind no matter where I go. Some trees I've spent time with on or near my property have developed a bond with me. Though their physical bodies are rooted to the ground, their spirits often show up when I go to a naturopathic healer for treatment. They give suggestions to the doctor for how to work with me, sometimes showing him hand holds and other techniques that he's never heard of before. The techniques always work. The trees also help him as he works with other clients.

One day the Healing Tree suffered trauma at the hands of an irrigation ditch rider. The ditch rider struck one of the Healing Tree's large branches with the shovel on a huge bulldozer, breaking it off. I told the doctor what had happened. He sat very still as he focused on the situation. Then he smiled. "The Healing Tree just sent a ley line to me so I could send energy to him," he said. After he sent the energy, the Healing Tree became an active part of our session, providing help to me even though he had been injured earlier that day. Such is the generosity and strength of spirit that trees offer us.

When I work with people who come to me for alternative healing sessions, the trees help me to stay grounded, and they give me other assistance. For example, if I forget to say a prayer asking for help at the beginning of a session, they are quick to remind me that it's an important part of the process and needs to happen. I've also been aware of them standing at the feet or side of a client as they offer healing energy.

Take time to cultivate the tree phone tool. It will benefit both you and the trees.

NINTH TOOL - EXPERTS

This tool attracts experts from all walks of life to lend their specialized skills as needed. These experts come from different socio-economic groups and occupational fields, from differing levels of mental and emotional skill, from all age levels, from sources beyond Earth, and from human, animal and plant kingdoms.

These experts are sometimes our own guides or angels. They could be people from our town, from a nearby city, or from the other side of the world who just happen to show up when their abilities, insights or assistance are needed. A tree or other plant that has grown to trust us can offer amazing assistance and provide invaluable information.

If you find yourself in need of help, don't be surprised if somebody you don't know turns up to offer that assistance. In whatever way it occurs, God's unconditional love directs that help to you.

I was mowing the weeds on an undeveloped lot on our church property one afternoon, feeling tired, thirsty and at the end of my strength. Another church member had spent the morning mowing one side of our property, and I'd taken over shortly before noon. There were many weeds still to mow, and I was too exhausted to finish the job. I wiped sweat from my forehead, then made one last turn around the lot. The rest of the mowing, I decided, would have to wait for another day.

As I rounded a corner with the lawnmower, something on the edge of my peripheral vision caught my attention. I turned to see a man on a huge riding lawnmower mowing the weeds ten feet away from me. He cropped them faster than I could have with my push lawnmower in the next hour. Over the sound of my lawnmower, I hadn't heard him. Where had he come from?

A woman emerged from a nearby pickup with a cold bottle of water. She handed it to me. I guzzled it down. The man, she told me, was a landscaper and handyman. As he drove around town on his way to various landscaping jobs that day, he had seen us mowing. He decided to lend a hand free of charge. Five minutes later, the weeds were gone, and the property looked better than it had in ages.

Experts such as that generous landscaper often appear when we are at our most desperate. They offer their help, then move on. We never forget their kindness, and they build within us a knowing that divine grace is at work in our lives.

TENTH TOOL - AMBASSADORS

The ambassadors tool is used by those who are skilled at helping people develop better relationships with each other. They show up when the time is right to intervene, when unrest is in the air, or when a person can no longer cope with a situation.

These ambassadors don't limit themselves to individuals having disagreements. If there is a political hotspot, a natural disaster, an outbreak of disease, a misunderstanding that spurs anger and thoughts of war between nations, they go into action. They may be human or angelic helpers, but their appearance provides a catalyst to promote peace and positive change.

They often don't call attention to themselves, and they use their skills in humble ways. Sometimes they don't seem to do anything at all. Late one night a single mother was driving home from an exhausting day at work. Her feet were swollen and purple from standing all day, but she knew she couldn't rest yet. There would be supper to fix for her young son when she got home, and she would need to help him with his homework. Sleeping in the passenger seat of the car was a friend she had made room for in her small apartment. That friend faced daunting challenges of her own. Her husband had recently been jailed, and she'd lost custody of her children, but she remained determined to somehow piece her life back together.

The single mother felt overwhelmed by all the responsibilities in her life. Would she ever find a less physically demanding job? Would she ever have time to take care of her own needs? As she drove, her eyes caught movement near the side of the road. She gasped when she saw a man walking on the shoulder. Long dark curly hair swirled around his shoulders, and the coat he wore looked like a robe. Wakened by the gasp, her friend bolted upright and demanded to know what was happening. "That man!" the driver exclaimed. "He looked like Jesus."

Her friend caught a glimpse of the slender man striding along. Indeed, he did bear a slight resemblance to Jesus. Who he really was the two women never knew, but seeing him lifted their spirits. When they got home, they completed their evening tasks with lighter hearts. They had been touched by an ambassador of hope who never made eye contact or exchanged a single word with them.

Such is the nature of this tool. It is often used in unique ways, in unexpected places, and by people who just "happen" to be passing through.

CHAPTER 4

PROTECTION TOOLS

We are surrounded by many kinds of protection. When we are children, our parents do their best to protect us from harmful situations. They teach us how to stay away from hot stoves, sharp knives, moving automobiles and other things that could be dangerous. As adults, we generally do a pretty good job of protecting ourselves. But unforeseen events, such as accidents, fires, or criminal activity can put us in harm's way.

Though many of us don't often think about it, there are challenges in the non-physical realm as well. If you walk into a room where people have been arguing, you may sense tension, a heavy feeling that pollutes the space. You might take on that tension without intending to just because you've been exposed to it.

If you have a strong desire to be of assistance to others, you may be more likely to take on their emotional baggage without realizing it. That's because you want to fix their problems yourself instead of depending on divine guidance to direct you. When a judgment or criticism enters your mind, more often than not it doesn't originate with you. It's likely that you've picked it up from an individual or a group of people without realizing it.

If you visit a long ago battlefield, pass the scene of an old crime, or enter a motel room in which an angry, depressed or addicted person once stayed, you may feel the heavy energy that still surrounds those places. If you are near an acquaintance or stranger who feels out of sorts, you can be affected by their angry, depressed or guilty emotions without realizing it even though their emotions have nothing to do with you.

Other people's false beliefs may have an effect on you and influence the way you view the world. Perhaps a relative once told you that you were no good and would never amount to anything. Maybe you read a book or article, saw a movie or television show, or visited social media sites that led you to adopt or strengthen a prejudice. Perhaps a teacher, friend or parent, whether knowingly or not, led you to believe something about yourself or someone else that wasn't true.

As you go through a day, the emotions of other people can affect you in spite of your best intentions. It's important to protect yourself from those influences so you don't clutter up your own energy system. Learning not to take on the drama of their stories is an important skill to master. Even if you succeed, you are not always immune to the heavy energy that contaminates the atmosphere around them. Installing a strong shield against negative influences will keep you healthier and make life more pleasant for you. Some of the tools offer shield-like qualities.

The shield of unconditional love can help with that. It's not one of the protection tools mentioned in this chapter, but it's an additional one that you can install yourself. Imagine the light of God's unconditional love filling and surrounding you like a strong, protective shield. It contains many colors that resonate well with you. Choose whatever colors make you feel strong, secure, and cherished. Imagine floating out through the top of your head high up into the heavens. Wrap the top part of that shield around a sturdy support beam there that will never break. Test it to be sure it's firmly attached. Then float down, reenter your body through the top of your head, and travel down through your body until you exit through your feet into the Earth.

Imagine taking the bottom part of that shield with you until you reach the center of the Earth. Find there an anchor so strong that nothing can budge it. Wrap the end of your shield around that anchor. Test it to be sure the attachment is strong. Then float back up into your body through your feet. See yourself surrounded by the strong, secure shield, and know that you are safe, cocooned in unconditional love.

Many of the protection tools in this chapter point to the truth of our divine nature which is perfect and has nothing to fear. Sometimes what we need protection from most is our own set of false beliefs that convince us we have limitations and weaknesses, making us vulnerable to attack.

As Lesson 135 in *A Course in Miracles, Workbook for Students,* points out, "A sense of threat is an acknowledgment of an inherent weakness; a belief that there is danger which has power to call on you to make appropriate defense. The world is based on this insane belief. And all its structures, all its thoughts and doubts, its penalties and heavy armaments, its legal definitions and its codes, its ethics and its leaders and its gods, all serve but to preserve its sense of threat. For no one walks the world in armature but must have terror striking at his heart."[6]

Our divine essence is so powerful, so loving, perfect and unchangeable that we don't need the protections we think we do. But until we remember who we really are, the protective tools provide crutches for us to help reduce our fears, which someday we will recognize are unfounded.

---

[6] A Course in Miracles, *Foundation for Inner Peace,* Mill Valley, CA, 1996. *Workbook for Students,* Lesson 135, pp. 252 and 253.

In many ways, we are like children who are scared of the dark, so our loving parents provide us with a night light to make us feel safe. Protection tools also help to lessen the fear while pointing us to the truth that, in reality, we have nothing to fear because we are holy children of God, "free of all limits, safe and healed and whole."[7]

As I spent time meditating with the trees, the protection tools that emerged over several weeks sometimes surprised me. Though they weren't what I had expected, they are all worth considering. They are offered from a place of loving support and a desire to help us remember who we really are. Perhaps you will find one or two that work well for you.

FIRST TOOL - BACK SHIELD

When this tool was revealed to me, I felt it being placed securely into my back. Shaped like a star, it fit perfectly into a space that had the same contours. Once installed, it became a shield that protected me from anyone who spoke unkind words about me or made harmful plans behind my back.

I suspect this tool comes in its own unique shape for each person, representing an interest, hobby or affinity for something. Certain kinds of trees are especially good at providing this type of protection. If you cultivate a relationship with a Russian olive tree, you may discover that the spirit of the tree follows you around, guarding your back.

One Russian olive, the Rear Guard Tree, is especially adept at this. During sleep, if I travel to other countries or other galaxies without consciously being aware of what I'm doing, the Rear Guard Tree accompanies me, keeping me safe, watching my back.

---

[7] *Ibid*. Lesson 97, p. 173

If you don't have a shield, such as the one described in the introduction to this chapter, you could be more affected by other people's negative energy and attitudes. When a young man with challenges on the job came to me for Reiki, he had so much energy congestion that it was hard to clear. As I tried to identify the cause of the problem, my attention kept going to his upper back. Something there gave him great difficulty. I drew the Reiki power symbol on his back, but the energy congestion remained. I drew it again, but still there was no change. Finally, when I drew it a third time, in my mind's eye, I saw a monkey fly off his back. With that mental picture came the understanding that three people at work were attacking him behind his back. Once the monkey was gone and, along with it, the influence of those three people, I filled that space with the energy of unconditional love, more powerful than anything else there is. Then the energy flowing through his body felt smooth and clear.

Ask your angels and spirit guides to install a back shield tool for you. We can be susceptible to verbal attacks from people, usually behind our backs. If we are honest with ourselves, most of us would have to admit that we have been guilty of backbiting too.

The back shield tool will help you navigate more safely through the challenges of daily living, and it may be a reminder not to speak unkindly of others. Engaging in backbiting is a form of attack. It's not healthy for the person being attacked, and it isn't good for the attacker either. Anytime we attack someone else, we are really attacking ourselves. We're all connected, all part of the whole, so anything that affects one person affects the other as well.

SECOND TOOL - BRACELET OF LIGHT

This non-physical jewelry looks soft and weighs next to nothing. When you put it around your wrist, it emits light, which surrounds you like a shield. This light vibrates at the frequency of unconditional love. It protects you from any harmful influence.

While it wraps you in protection, its light waves also beam a message to others that light removes anything negative and that they too can have a light bracelet. All they have to do is ask for divine assistance to get one. Angels are standing by who can hardly wait to be of service.

But, like any of the tools, to get it you have to ask for it, and you must be willing to receive it and use it.

This light bracelet cannot be used as a weapon against anyone, because it is spun from unconditional love. If people understand the value of the bracelet and want it to promote their own agenda at the expense of others, it will not be effective. Nothing, not even our deepest longings and highest ambitions, are greater than God's unconditional love. Everything that does not vibrate at that highest of all frequencies is absorbed by unconditional love and transformed into it.

You cannot use a protection tool that contains the light of unconditional love in a way that will harm another person. The light will change everything it touches into unconditional love. When you wear the bracelet of light, whatever heavy or negative energy others may send against you will be absorbed by light and transformed into unconditional love.

THIRD TOOL - THE SPIRE

As I perceive it, this tool has a tall, thin, triangular shape, taller and thinner than most pyramids. It has a base deep in

Mother Earth. The widest part of the spire anchors into the center of the Earth. From there, it travels upward, enters the bottoms of your feet and travels into your body. As it travels upward, its tip forms a peak that emerges through the top of your head. Its point travels upward, anchoring firmly into divinity.

The spire tool brings protection, helps you to stay focused and grounded, and makes you aware of the nourishing flow of energy from both Earth and God. Its narrow shape makes it less visible to negative energies that otherwise might cast a heavy influence over your thoughts. Those negative energies are really illusions, but they have become real in our minds. Fear of them can stop people in their tracks.

As this tool paves a clear pathway for positive energy, it helps you to be more conscious of inspiration and of answers to troubling questions. Even if you forget that the spire tool is yours to use, it continues to be available to you. All you have to do is ask.

FOURTH TOOL - THE BOUNCER

The bouncer tool has the appearance of a rubbery, gel-like substance that ripples and sparkles. It completely surrounds you. If people send you negative thoughts that seek to imbed themselves under your skin like poisonous darts, the bouncer tool lets them bounce off of you as though you were a trampoline. They tumble down to Mother Earth, where they are absorbed and transformed into something positive.

If you ever feel that someone has tried to splatter you with a negative thought, call on the bouncer tool. No matter what is thrown at you, it can't stick. It will bounce off. You can let Mother Earth absorb the negativity, or you can ask the bouncer tool to return the negative thought to the sender with unconditional love. Love is more powerful than anything else. It can dissolve anything that isn't healthy for you and transform it into something positive.

FIFTH TOOL - SUPPLY TRUCK

Like a huge truck covered with camouflage paint, this tool contains the essence of invisibility jackets, secret caves, full-body armor and other equipment to help you survive in a hostile environment. The list of supplies is as bottomless as your imagination and as limitless as your fertile mind to improvise. The supply truck tool is another way of helping you to remember that you are completely safe, because you are divine, a holy child of God.

If you feel in need of something, see yourself reaching into the truck and drawing out whatever you need. Create the things you need with the power of your imagination. Think those things into existence. Though this tool may sound too simplistic, something a playful child might dream up, don't discount its power to help you manifest what you need.

Invisibility jackets and secret caves sound like they come from the world of make believe, but don't underestimate what is available to you in your supply truck full of unusual and amazing tools. If you dig down far enough and deep enough, you may find a note from God saying, "I love you. You are safe. There is nothing to fear. But until you know that truth deep within your heart, I will continue to offer you supplies to ease your fear."

SIXTH TOOL - WINGS

One of the easiest ways to use this tool is to imagine a set of wings. Close your eyes and see beautiful wings in your mind. They could be made of feathers, paper, clouds, or whatever you want to envision. As you focus on the wings, notice how your mind begins to quiet. Soon you will rise above the jangle of negative influences, emotions or thoughts that affect you every day. In their place you will notice peacefulness. A feeling of calm will settle over you.

Whenever you use this tool, you can imagine the same set of wings or a different set made of material that will help you rise above whatever challenges you face in that moment. The more you use the image of wings, the more quickly you will find yourself settling into a state of meditation. From this place of relaxation, you will have easier access to ideas for solving problems that you face. Your stress level will fall, and you will discover that you can fly to a peaceful, restorative place on the wings of your imagination.

One way to use the wings tool is by practicing the Essence Technique developed by my best friend when she had significant physical and emotional challenges. It works like this. If you are having a problem with a person or thing, such as a toxic reaction to a chemical or food, meditate for a few moments, focus on your breath and clear your mind of any distractions. Then ask permission to see the essence of that person or thing. You will likely begin to sense something. You might see pictures in your mind, hear sounds, smell, taste, or touch something that will help you understand the essence of the person or thing.

Its essence may surprise you. In my experience it has always been something so beautiful and amazing that I would never have imagined something so problematic could be so wonderful. That deepened understanding will act as wings, helping you rise above and see beyond whatever difficulties you were having with that person or thing. You may find yourself entering a state of gratitude in which your whole outlook changes and you discover new possibilities and solutions as you gain a deeper level of understanding.

What's really happening is that you are recognizing the Oneness that connects you all. You and all that is troubling you are, in reality, part of the whole. When you can see divinity in the person or thing with which you struggle, it becomes wrapped in the light of unconditional love. That light transforms both of you into pure love, where disagreements and difficulties melt away.

SEVENTH TOOL - ROOT TALK

This tool provides a form of thought travel that links you to trees around the world. Trees have their own forms of communication. They send warnings that give other trees a chance to protect themselves. They also send each other requests for help and provide encouraging messages. Trees link with each other across thousands of miles through this underground root system.

These messages come in the form of energy impulses that surge from root to root, even jumping across canyons, oceans, and deserts to connect with the next available root. Trees also sometimes link with each other through humans. If you visit one part of the country, a tree can deposit a thought into your energy system. You may not realize you're carrying a message from a tree, but when you walk near a tree back home, that tree will receive the message and pass it on to other trees.

Trees can create ley lines, or energy pathways, between them and you so that you can send them energy when they need it. You can send them energy in many ways, but when a tree needs help fast, it may send a ley line to you on which you can send it energy. This usually happens during times of great stress or trauma to the tree.

Trees pass on messages about you to each other. If you have developed a relationship of trust with them, they will communicate that information with other trees. Don't be surprised if you're away from home and realize that trees you've never seen before are trying to get your attention. They may want you to acknowledge them or pray for them. They may want you to carry a message to another tree for them. Often they are in distress or feel abandoned, and a little attention from you will give them the strength and encouragement to carry on.

When trees learn how to handle difficult situations, through their roots they pass what they learned to other trees in similar situations. That's one way they help each other through tough times.

EIGHTH TOOL - SMART SPADE

I call this tool a smart spade, because it's a bit like a non-physical smart phone or computer. It can be programmed to draw from the Earth whatever you need. It's a visual aid to help you manifest, or create. However, it will work only if what you ask for resonates with the purpose you set for yourself when you embarked on this life's journey.

Imagine that you can hold it in your hand and punch in commands and instructions on a mini-keyboard. When you can see it in your mind, hear the sounds that the keys make as they move under your fingers or just sense that it's there. Begin to play with the possibilities it offers. It will help to protect you against doubt. It will strengthen your ability to believe and to feel that what you want is on its way to you.

Imagine it drawing from the Earth all the protection, wisdom and knowledge that you need for whatever situation you face. The more clearly you can imagine what you want and the more joy you can feel about having it, the more likely it will be to manifest – as long as it resonates with your life's purpose.

NINTH TOOL - TRANSITIONER

Like a butterfly transforming as it emerges from a cocoon, this tool allows you to move from adversity and fear of failure to opportunity and success. It helps your mind to transition from a dark, negative way of thinking to a light, positive one. It can provide healing from the pain of loss or disappointment.

To use the tool, focus on the light of God's unconditional love. Imagine a beautiful place, or think of a person you love to be around. Fill your mind with those thoughts. Give yourself time to experience the joy and delight those thoughts bring. The more you focus on thoughts of love and beauty, the easier it is to transition out of the effects of tragedy or despair.

Make this tool look like anything you'd like. It could be a room the size of a small sauna. Imagine yourself entering it and finding a comfortable place to sit. See yourself wrapped in a huge, fluffy towel that represents love and beauty. Or, instead of a sauna, it could be as small as the size of a remote control for your television. When you don't like the thoughts and feelings that rise up in you, click the remote control and change the channel to something more pleasant.

As silly as this tool sounds, the more you practice using it the more able you will be to switch your thinking from unhappy thoughts to pleasant ones. It helps you be more mindful of focusing on the moment at hand where you don't dwell on aggravations of past or worry about the future. If you have to be somewhere that you don't want to be, pretend that you're glad to be there and pretty soon you'll find yourself in a more positive frame of mind.

TENTH TOOL -- SHOES

If you have a difficult ordeal to face, these shoes can help you walk through troubles ahead. Your challenges could be as difficult to traverse as a hot bed of coals, sharp rocks, flowing lava, or ice so cold it could give your feet frostbite.

Imagine strapping on a pair of shoes with an energy field so strong that it creates a cushion between you and your troubles. That energy field spreads way beyond where you're standing. It provides a wide circle of protection.

Put your artistic mind in gear and see yourself painting exotic, classy or durable shoes with a wild array of colors and designs. Get your creative juices flowing. As you immerse yourself in your prolific imagination, you may discover ideas flooding your mind with solutions to the problems you face that, until now, seemed too huge to resolve.

CHAPTER 5

LEADERSHIP TOOLS

People who think that leadership involves taking control and forcing their agenda on others will be disappointed by these tools. They are much more subtle and based on a genuine appreciation of others and a desire to let them shine.

Leadership involves helping those on your team or in your business capture the essence of what's needed to create a magnificent product, event or service that no one could have developed as well on their own. It's about inspiring and encouraging others, motivating them, and paying attention to their opinions and ideas. It's also about seeing the big picture, the overall purpose or mission, and understanding how to bring that big picture into reality. The best leaders can do that while they invite suggestions from others about how to get there.

The most effective leaders don't call attention to themselves. They call attention to the hard working, creative, insightful people with whom they work, and they build up their associates' confidence to accomplish even greater endeavors. They also see people without judgment. They notice others' strengths and offer them positions that will allow those strengths to shine, but they do it without putting people down for the things they don't do so well.

FIRST TOOL - APPRECIATION

Think of this tool as a beautiful necklace strung with many sparkling, precious stones.

They carry within them the energy pattern of appreciation. When you are in a leadership role, imagine wearing that necklace around your neck. Every time you touch one of those stones, you increase its ability to help you express appreciation.

When you want to show people how much you appreciate them, imagine touching one of those stones and focusing on the energy pattern of appreciation. That kind of visualization may help you think of creative and meaningful ways to show others how much you value them and their contributions. If you prefer to use something other than the image of a necklace, tune into whatever sense helps you feel most receptive to spiritual guidance.

One of the finest ways to show appreciation is to compliment a store clerk who has been especially helpful to you. To give it an extra zing, make the compliment while the clerk's boss is listening. In addition to leaving a good tip, thank waiters and waitresses for the fine service they provide. It only takes a few seconds of your time, but they will remember it. If they've been having a stressful day, it will help them feel more hopeful and valued.

Don't stop there with your appreciation. Thank your spouse, children, friends, teachers, and others for the kind and helpful things they do for you and others.

You will think of additional ways to show your appreciation as you focus on seeing the positive aspects in others. Don't be surprised that as you show your appreciation, people will appreciate you more as well.

SECOND TOOL - VALUE

Wherever you go, do the best you can to promote a peaceful atmosphere. Instead of taking offense when someone says something that pushes your buttons, take a deep breath and ask God, your angels and spirit helpers to give you patience and insight. Think of at least one good thing about the person who pushed your buttons. Recognize the talents that person has to offer. When they do something that upsets you, take time to understand the valuable service they perform. In spite of how aggravated they can make you feel, they are on some level helping you to remember and reclaim the amazing person you are. When you see them as your teachers and helpers, you will see them in a different light and be able to respond to them in a more positive way. As you practice seeing value in everyone, even them, you can learn to let what they did or what they said about you roll like water off a duck's back.

When we respond in anger, sarcasm, or disrespect, we set in motion negative energy that affects the person we aim it towards and hurts us as well. That energy is present until we change our frame of mind and focus on more positive, healthy thoughts. Any time we devalue someone else, we put an energetic ball and chain around our own leg that we must drag along until we learn to change our thoughts and actions. Not only that, but when we fail to see the value in others, we fail to see our own value because on some level we are all one, all cut from the same cloth, all children of the same Creator.

It's easy for us to fly off the handle when our buttons get pushed. If we can treat those moments as learning experiences, we can discover what areas in our personalities still need to be healed. I was at a conference luncheon once when I saw someone trying to help another person at our table lift a heavy pitcher and pour water into a glass. The angle of her approach made the task difficult. When I suggested using a different angle for pouring, I was met with resistance.

Indignation boiled up in me for a few seconds as I thought, "I was just trying to help!" But then it occurred to me that no one had asked for my opinion. They probably didn't want it or think they needed it. I took a deep breath and let my indignation drain away. Those people had taught me a valuable lesson. Something in me felt the need to make unsolicited suggestions and was asking to be healed. It wasn't their attitude, but my own that needed tweaking. Sometimes we must value others enough to let them do what they want to do even if we think they're making a mistake. We deny them the opportunity to grow and learn if we're always trying to be the fix-it person.

Some people seem naturally gifted at valuing others. I watched a magistrate court judge in action one day. She carried out her job with style, humor, and efficiency. All the plaintiffs and defendants in that courtroom left feeling that they had been heard and that their feelings were important. Her recent retirement was a loss to the community, because she had an extraordinary ability to recognize the good in every individual no matter what the situation.

THIRD TOOL - ONENESS

This tool helps you remember what it feels like to be connected to everyone and everything. Imagine looking into a round pool of water along with other people who are standing at the edge peering into it. Trees, bushes, and woodland animals are also reflected in the pool.

As you imagine seeing everyone's bodies reflected in the water, watch ripples begin to form on the pool's surface. The ripples turn each reflection into images that start to blend into each other. You are one with all of them, and they are one with you.

This act of blending into a whole allows God to work through all of you to do what is needed in the moment. If you're a parent, boss, club president, or the organizer of a community yard sale, you may feel the weight of the world sitting on your shoulders. What decisions should you make? How should you solve this problem or that disagreement?

When you sense the Oneness that unites us all, it becomes apparent that you don't have to know all the answers or have all the solutions. If you have no idea what to do, turn to others in your group for help. Ask them for suggestions. Recognize that someone else in the group, in your family, or among your friends may have an excellent approach to whatever problem needs to be fixed. You don't lessen your image in other people's eyes when you ask for help. You enhance it, because you are recognizing the contributions they have to offer. In this way, you are forging a stronger, more powerful whole.

Let God use the blending of your beings to orchestrate events. As a leader, you bear responsibility, but you don't have to stand alone. Turn to others for help. Ask God for guidance, and watch to see how the Oneness that unites us all results in fabulous ideas and creative solutions.

Once we remember our Oneness, we recall that our connection unites us with all the possibilities and potential that exist everywhere in the universe. We are connected with divine wisdom in a constant, uninterrupted flow. When we realize that, we discover what an asset the Oneness tool is to our leadership

FOURTH TOOL - ATTENTION

Paying attention to others is one way of honoring them. In this way, you show that what they are doing has worth and that you consider it valuable enough to notice.

Bosses, parents, and others in positions of authority often don't have much time to use this tool because of their own demanding jobs. But even a few seconds spent noticing how well someone performs a skill, handles a client, offers an idea, or does their chores will reap many benefits. You are affirming their value and showing that you care.

All too often, the effort and care that people put into doing the best they can goes either unnoticed or unacknowledged. When someone does notice what you do, it brightens your day. You may remember a time when someone not only paid attention to what you were doing, but made a point of telling you what a good job you'd done. Those moments of recognition etch themselves in your memories and carry you over rough times when your responsibilities seem overwhelming. During those tough moments, you can recall the attention someone gave you, the recognition you received for a job well done, the hug of thanks someone gave you. That makes it worth the effort to keep trying, to put one foot in front of the other even when life seems incredibly difficult.

Several years ago, a visitor at our house sometimes made it a point to sit in the kitchen while he watched me prepare a meal. It was his way of paying attention and honoring the work that went into cooking. He wasn't comfortable in the role of helping to make a tossed salad, setting the table, or peeling potatoes. He found his own way of taking notice that resonated with him. There were times when I could have used his help, but I recognized that he was doing his best to help in his own way.

People have different ways of offering their help. It is a leader's task to recognize the value in each act and to courteously suggest other ways of helping when the need arises.

A girl in the elementary school where I once worked as a counselor often came to talk with me about the challenges she faced at home, especially with her mother's choice of an abusive boyfriend. At the end of the school year, she put a thank you card in my school mail box along with a beautiful pair of ear rings. I didn't find them until after she left for the summer. I lost contact with her and wasn't able to thank her for her gift. Years later, when my husband and I stopped at a restaurant for an evening meal, she saw me and made a point of saying hello. She worked as a waitress there. She told me her life had dramatically improved. Her mother now provided a bedrock of support for her and her young child. The once seemingly insurmountable family challenges had been resolved. I thanked her for the ear rings she had given me so long ago. Her hand flew to her mouth, and she giggled. There was a bounce in her step as she resumed her work.

When you pay attention to others and tell them you noticed their good work, their positive attitude, or their kind gesture, you brighten their day. That small act of yours may spur them to smile at someone else, who will show kindness to another person in a never ending circle of good will that has the potential to change the world for the better.

FIFTH TOOL - RESPONSIBILITY

Have you ever worked for someone who made you feel so important and valued that you loved coming to work and shouldering the responsibilities of your job? It takes a skillful leader to create an atmosphere in which people feel so personally invested that they proudly take responsibility for helping to make the business or the project a rousing success.

This tool involves creating that kind of positive, nurturing atmosphere. People are more willing to take responsibility if they feel valued and if they can see that their contribution is appreciated and considered useful and helpful. They will feel even more valued if you find a way to point out their accomplishments when other people hear what you say.

No matter how much you encourage others and give credit to them, the responsibility tool will not work well if people have so much to do that they feel constantly exhausted and burned out. Make sure you aren't taking on too much work yourself. If you are, you reduce your effectiveness. By the same token, those who work for you or with you shouldn't shoulder more than their share of obligations either. When people feel frequently overwhelmed, they stop finding joy in their work and start to feel a sense of obligation, burden and, sometimes, resentment. That's when people make mistakes, decide to drop out, or become depressed. Businesses, organizations, service projects and other endeavors begin to fail if that kind of atmosphere persists.

One of the best ways to encourage responsibility is to let people take short breaks at work when they need them, a few minutes here and there. That helps them to recharge their batteries so they can be more responsible and productive with a positive attitude.

Often, people work hard to do the best job they can, but results are mediocre or worse because the plan of action or the system needs to be tweaked to create better results. If, for example, people are working to create a toy car that turns corners easily without rolling over, they can't do a good job if they're given faulty instructions or square tires. If you take the time to listen to people when they voice concerns and suggestions, together you will discover solutions that can turn a failing project or business into a rousing success. Acknowledging the value of people and what they have to offer goes a long way toward promoting a healthy sense of responsibility and a more productive workplace.

Tune into the nuts and bolts of how to use this tool by spending time in your favorite meditation or prayer spot. Focus on a specific situation. Ask how you can use the tool to be more responsible yourself or to nurture that quality in others. Then quiet your mind and listen to the answers that come. Ask your divine assistants to help you see clearly how to proceed. You may be directed to seek advice from an expert or to take certain steps on your own. Part of using the responsibility tool involves doing all you can yourself even though you may not be sure what to do. When you take that first step, divine assistance lends a hand, ideas flow, and solutions present themselves.

SIXTH TOOL - OBSERVE

To use this tool, you must be willing to check out all the angles, to carefully observe what is happening around you, and to adjust your point of view if necessary. When you can let go of your own beliefs about what needs to happen, you are more likely to discover methods of helping people work together in positive, responsible ways. Is Sally not able to perform well because she needs better equipment? Is Harold unable to concentrate because he's overwhelmed with a crisis at home? Does John fail to answer emails because he works best when someone talks with him face to face? Is Betty working hard but making little progress because the instructions she's being given are faulty or so complicated that they make no sense to her?

Sometimes employers and national leaders disguise themselves so they can go unrecognized to get a clearer picture of the challenges their employees or countrymen face. It helps them gain insight into how those people would do things better if given upgraded equipment, a more sensible work environment, or more realistic incentives.

This tool requires that you let go of the need to be right. It won't work unless you're willing to give up your theories about why things are happening and what makes people act the way they do in certain situations. Let go of judgment. Simply observe. That's when everything will come into focus, and you will begin to understand where the problems lie so you can find meaningful solutions.

SEVENTH TOOL - HUMILITY

This is a challenging tool for many people. You must be willing to admit that you need help, that you don't have all the answers. You can't juggle too many balls without dropping some of them. You don't have the same level of skills and abilities that some other people do. They could carry out a task in their area of expertise better than you if you would only give them the opportunity. It takes a wise person to know when to step aside and let someone else handle a task for which they are best suited.

With this tool, you can learn to stay in tune with your own needs. If you need some time off, take it. Admit that you can't hold the world up all by yourself. You can't go forever without a vacation. Do you need to take a day off to rest or handle a family issue? Do you need a few days to spend quality time with the people you love? Recognize your limitations, and get help or take time for yourself when you need it.

There's no shame in needing someone to assist you, in recognizing that you can't go forever without a break, or in seeking the help of a psychotherapist to navigate tough life issues. You cannot serve others well or be a good leader when you don't take good care of yourself. Be humble enough to admit when you need help.

EIGHTH TOOL - ENERGY BOOST

Everything is energy, and everything has a different vibrational frequency. One person may vibrate at a higher level than someone else. The higher your vibration, the more you will encounter loving, nurturing situations. The lower your vibration, the more you will live in a fear-based environment.

When you're upset about something, your energy tends to dip. When you're exhilarated, your energy climbs. If you feel sick, you don't have much energy at all. If you've gotten a salary increase, an award, or won the lottery, you bubble with positive energy.

Some people feel unhappy with themselves, so they create dissention or say mean things about someone else in an effort to make themselves feel less miserable. You can't change people or their attitudes, but you can control how you react to them. By keeping your own energy up, you help to boost the atmosphere around you.

At work, does Tom bad mouth Ed to you because Ed made a costly mistake? Listen, and then point out that we've all made mistakes. If it's appropriate, ask Ed what happened and how he thinks the problem can be fixed. Maybe you can help Tom and Ed work together better and learn to value each other more. In that way, Tom stops feeling angry and self-righteous, and Ed stops feeling guilty and harassed. As a result, both of their energies will be boosted, improving the atmosphere around you.

Boosting your energy can be easier than it sounds. Hang around people who make you feel positive. Listen to upbeat music. If you play a musical instrument, take time to practice it to maintain and improve your skills so you can keep enjoying the pleasure it gives you. Sing along to your favorite tunes whether or not you have a good voice. Doing so will lift your spirits and help you to breathe more deeply as you inhale oxygen to sing the next few words. Your body performs better when it's well oxygenated. If you like being surrounded by mountains or hills, hike along a mountain trail or explore hilly terrain. Walk near a river. Listen to the water bubble over rocks and swish through vegetation along the bank. Find a quiet place to pray or meditate even for a few minutes. Your spirits will start to rise, there will be a bounce in your step, and you will recognize that the vibrational frequency of your energy has just gone up.

NINTH TOOL - EYEGLASSES

Imagine putting on a pair of eyeglasses that will help you see the positive aspects of everyone. No matter how terrible their actions may be, when you look through these eyeglasses you can see even the tiniest speck of goodness in them. When you see that speck of goodness, focus on that. It will not only help you see another side of people, it will also help them to remember there are sparks of goodness within themselves. That remembering could help nurture positive qualities in them because you took time to see through positive lenses without judgment.

When you put on those imaginary eyeglasses, also take a look at yourself. Sometimes you're so hard on yourself that you fail to see your own goodness. Perhaps you take yourself to task for the tiniest mistakes or oversights. If that happens, tell yourself, "I'm sorry. Please forgive me for being so judgmental." Then add, "Thank you, I love you." Those phrases are variations of a Hawaiian method called

Ho'oponopono, which helps to erase the false beliefs in our subconscious mind and replace them with more positive, loving ones. Repeat the phrases, "I'm sorry, please forgive me, thank you, I love you," as often as you need to. When you say those words, you are speaking to that part of yourself that carries judgmental feelings and false beliefs about yourself. You are helping to erase those misconceptions. As you do that, something in you will start to heal, and it may begin to heal people around you as well.

Putting on those imaginary eyeglasses helps you to recognize that you and others are worthy people and that you can forgive yourself and them. You'll feel lighter if you let go of the weight of all those negative thoughts and attitudes you've been carrying around. Go ahead. Put on those imaginary eyeglasses and see the world in a brighter, happier light. You'll be surprised how much more productive you and the people in your life become.

TENTH TOOL - PRESENT MOMENT LIGHT

This tool is particularly powerful. It involves being in the present moment, free from distresses of the past and worries about the future. In present moment reality, you become aware of so much light and love surrounding you and expanding throughout the Earth, into the universe and beyond that you're aware of nothing else.

Eckhart Tolle, who wrote *The Power of Now,* briefly described how he moved from a place of misery, struggle, and desire to die into a state of bliss, love, and light. The intense mental suffering he felt when he woke up in the middle of the night shortly after his 29th birthday forced his consciousness to stop identifying with his unhappy, fearful self, which wasn't real, and to recognize his true nature, which is pure consciousness. When people told him they wanted what he had, he replied, "You have it already. You just can't feel it because your mind is making too much noise."[8]

You can access your true nature, in which you become aware of your connection with everything, only when the mind is still. One way to find that stillness is to spend some time in nature, focusing on a tree, a bush, a river, a rock, an animal, or a cloud in the sky. Let go of second guessing the past or trying to figure out the future. Just be in the present moment when your mind is no longer going a mile a minute. Instead, you are only aware of what is happening right now in this moment. If you're looking at a tree, notice the color of the leaves, how they flutter in the wind, the bark patterns on the tree trunk, the intricate designs made by the branches.

Experience the delight and beauty of your connection with the tree. Before you know it, you will sense the power of present moment light. As you feel renewed in that moment, you will take its peace and potential for healing with you into your everyday life. People who come in contact with you will feel calmer and more connected to the true essence of Oneness that connects us all. They, in turn, will spread that peacefulness to others.

Only a few seconds spent in present moment light makes this expansion of love and peace possible. It can be hard to stay in the present moment, but if you achieve it for just a few seconds, you will experience its power.

Once we had several geese, which we allowed to wander on our property. It was fun to watch them waddle down a dirt path, grubbing for bugs or racing after flying insects. I became

---

[8] Eckhart, Tolle, *The Power of Now,* Namaste Publishing and New World Library, Novato, CA, 1999, p. 6

so fascinated with their antics one afternoon that I watched them for almost five minutes, mesmerized by their movements. Neither the past nor the future was real to me in those moments, only my sense of oneness with them. I felt rested and rejuvenated, and years later I still remember the peacefulness of that moment in time. Back then, I had no idea how powerful the ability to focus on the present moment can be. Now I'm more aware of the chain reaction we create by finding peace and calm right here, right now, in this present moment. It becomes contagious. People around us start to feel more tranquil too.

CHAPTER 6

BUSINESS TOOLS

Finding success in business involves, among other things, wise planning, financial and people skills, healthy attitudes, adroit advice, and luck. However, the business tools I learned from the tree didn't stress any of those things. They were both unexpected and delightful. Though I'm aware that as an individual it's important for me to stay grounded, I had never thought of applying the concept of being grounded to a business. Yet, it makes great sense. When a business is focused and connected to its own needs and the needs of its clients, it is more likely to be successful.

If people who are thinking about starting a new business build these tools into their plans, might they discover a higher rate of success? I would like to think so. Whether these tools make sense to most businesses or not, they can add elements of fun and stability to just about any organization.

FIRST TOOL - JOY

When I first became aware of this tool, it resembled a beautiful star surrounded by fleecy circular white clouds above a lush, green meadow with a winding stream. The atmosphere felt healthy, calm, and harmonious. All my needs were met in that atmosphere. Abundance and joy pervaded everything.

When a harmonious atmosphere like that can be sustained in a business, joy is bound to follow. It's also more likely to promote success. Customers who sense that joy are apt to return to it again and again because of how they feel there.

It's essential to realize that the business isn't as much about you is at is about meeting your customers' needs. When you do that well, you bring joy to both you and your clients.

Joy can bubble up when you think of how to solve a problem you've had that others also face. An example of such a business is The Pet Loo. Begun in Australia, the business provides a way for pet owners to let their dogs relieve themselves any time. The idea caught on, and the product has spread to other countries. The Pet Loo is just a square of fake grass sitting on top of a waste containment system that you can put in your laundry room, basement, balcony or somewhere else convenient. [9] It's helpful when a pet owner is at work and can't take the dog out. It's also great for saving an owner sleep in the middle of the night when the dog needs to do its job. Instead of going outside, it can use the Pet Loo. Elderly people who have trouble walking benefit because they no longer have to take their pets out several times a day. They can gauge their pet's walking activity to their own physical stamina.

When someone solves a problem for other people and, in the process, makes a successful business out of it, they can bring joy into a lot of people's – and dogs' – lives. If you want to start a successful business, think of something that brings you joy and find a way to share it with others. Once the business is on its feet, find ways to keep the joy alive. When customers share how your product or service has brought them joy, savor that story, share it, and know that you're doing something so important that it's changing people's lives for the better.

---

[9]*thepetloo.us/; moneycrashers.com/weird-successful-small-business-ideas; topnonprofits.com/examples/vision-statements*

SECOND TOOL – STAY GROUNDED

I have known for a long time that staying grounded is important for individuals, but I had never thought that businesses needed to be grounded. After all, a business is a thing, not a person. But through this tool I came to understand that everything needs a healthy balance between the planet on which it exists and its own divine nature.

In reality, business owners are the ones who need to stay grounded in the mission of their business. When they are grounded, the business is also well grounded. As they encourage their employees to be well grounded, the entire organization exudes better health. Customers like how it feels to visit the business. It has a satisfying, fulfilling atmosphere that brims with positive energy.

Some signs indicating solid grounding on the part of a business owner or employee are that they think creatively, they are dependable, compassionate and enthusiastic. They are motivated, curious, and confident, and they recover well from failure. Anytime you feel yourself deviating from those traits, stop and ground yourself. The business you own or work for is only as well-grounded as its people. Take a few seconds to focus on your connection to the Earth and to the things that made you start the company or that led you to work there.

Once you're refocused on what you consider important and valuable, you will feel and act more grounded, connected and committed to your business. You will make better decisions, treat people with greater kindness and respect, and recapture your sense of purpose. When that happens, watch how fast your business improves.

THIRD TOOL – INTERGALACTIC HIGHWAY

I thought this was a pretty crazy concept when I first

caught a glimpse of the tool. An intergalactic highway? Could anyone take that seriously? But the more I thought about it, the more sense it made. We are part of a gargantuan universe with trillions of planets and stars in our galaxy alone. Every planet, star, meteor, person, plant and animal is connected in this huge space.

If we can find a way to communicate on the intergalactic highway that connects us all, could we perhaps find beings who have already solved the problems we face, discovered the inventions we are struggling to create, written the songs and books that will bring hope to others, composed the music that will sooth troubled souls? They might be able to help us successfully deal with whatever challenges we encounter. What a vast source of knowledge and mentoring would become available to us if we could travel on the intergalactic highway!

To use this tool, while you're meditating or praying state the issue or problem you face. Then ask to be taken on the intergalactic highway to wherever in the universe someone exists who has solved that problem, faced that challenge, reached that goal. Be in the present moment as you seek for the answers. Unless you quiet your chattering mind, which can make you feel fearful, you may misunderstand what you're being taught. Don't judge what comes into your mind. Don't second guess it or doubt it. Any advice you glean on the intergalactic highway will be wrapped in unconditional love. Therefore, you will never receive advice that could harm anyone. If you do get such advice, know that you've gotten in your own way. Take a little more time to pray or meditate. Then try stepping onto the intergalactic highway again.

Focus on what you're learning, bring it back and play with the ideas until they feel right to you and fit your needs. Let go of the fear that you won't remember what you were taught, because what you need to know will resurface at the right time. You may be amazed by how many challenges you overcome when you use this tool.

FOURTH TOOL - PORTALS

When decisions are made and actions are taken that result in costly mistakes, they can create a huge setback for a business. But what if there was another way to look at those mistakes? What if they could be turned into an avenue paved with success?

A mother fox once built her den on the side of our pasture not far from an irrigation ditch. It seemed to be a safe location. When the cubs were old enough, they ventured out of the hole and curiously watched people who hiked along the bank. They weren't afraid. Their mother, on the other hand, was alarmed that her cubs had been spotted by two friends of mine who walked along the bank with their dogs. She abandoned the den and moved her cubs somewhere else. My friends never saw the foxes again, but they told me how wise and caring the mother was about the safety of her little ones. They believed she dug a more secluded den where her cubs could grow to maturity.

That's what the portal tool is all about. It's about taking advantage of the abandoned holes, the wrong location choices, the decisions that lead to costly disasters. What if those decisions, accidents, and events could lead to success? What if you could travel through the portals created by those seeming disasters to discover great truths, alternative ideas, and deep understandings that would not have been available to you in any other way?

We can't literally crawl through an animal's abandoned hole to diagnose their mistakes and recommend different solutions. But we can use abandoned holes, severed tree limbs, anything that provides a pathway into Mother Earth, into that intuitive, nurturing, creative part of ourselves, to explore the pros and cons of any issue. As we explore, we can examine our mistakes and discover what we could have done better so we find success the next time around.

To use this tool, imagine exploring a hole made by a mistake. Let it take you to the end of the hole, which opens into a huge art gallery that you create with your imagination. Each painting and sculpture captures that hole, that severed tree limb, that disastrous decision in a new light. Study each work of art to find within it the discovery, invention, or innovative idea that, when properly applied, will lead to resounding success.

Countless mistakes have led to groundbreaking discoveries. For example, naval engineer Richard Jones was trying to make a meter designed to monitor power on naval battleships when he dropped a tension spring. It kept bouncing after it hit the ground. Instead of getting upset, he let his creative mind come up with the slinky, which has been a favorite children's toy for decades.

Scientist Sir Alexander Fleming was searching for a wonder drug that could cure diseases when he noticed that a contaminated Petri dish he had discarded contained a mold that dissolved all the bacteria around it. Intrigued, Fleming grew the mold in a Petri dish by itself and discovered it contained the powerful antibiotic penicillin.

Raytheon Corporation engineer Percy Spencer was conducting radar related research with a new vacuum tube when he realized the heat from the experiments was melting a candy bar in his pocket. He didn't let the melting candy bar bother him. Instead, he put some popcorn into the tube. When it started to pop, he knew he had discovered a revolutionary device. As a result, the microwave oven was born.

When Spencer Silver, a researcher in 3M Laboratories, tried to make a strong adhesive, he created instead an adhesive weaker than what already existed. He could stick it to objects, then pull it off without leaving a mark. It wasn't what he'd been trying to achieve, so he shelved the idea. Years later when a colleague spread the substance on little pieces of paper to mark his place in a choir hymn book, Post-it notes were born. They have found their way into millions of homes and businesses around the world.[10]

Don't sell yourself short when you make a mistake. That mistake might unlock an important invention, idea or cure that could change the lives of millions for the better. Businesses that promote that kind of thinking are likely to find themselves on the creative forefront that could earn them millions of dollars. Explore the portals of your mistakes. Don't be afraid to recognize them as opportunities just waiting to be discovered.

FIFTH TOOL - PUZZLES

Some people are especially gifted at solving puzzles. Spread a 1,000-piece puzzle in front of them, and they can have it put together in an hour or two. For the rest of us, it might take several days.

Being able to take seemingly fragmented pieces of information or ideas and fitting them together into a sensible, dynamic, workable plan is an amazing gift. Being able to bring that plan to fruition so it becomes a usable product is an even more amazing gift.

---

10 *businessinsider.com/these-10-inventions-were-made-by-mistake-2010-11?op=1/#e-slinky-1*

This tool is all about fitting odd pieces together so they become a productive whole. What someone discarded as junk could become a priceless treasure to those who know how to use this tool. It requires a new way of looking at things. Let go of judgment, put aside preconceived ideas, and side-step conventional thinking. If you can do that, you will begin to see that everything has value, no matter how seemingly irrelevant.

George Crum, a chef at the Carey Moon Lake House in Saratoga Springs, New York, wouldn't have discovered potato chips if he had thrown away a plate of potatoes that a customer didn't like. When the customer kept sending the potatoes back because he wanted them sliced thinner and fried longer, Crum's temper began to climb. Instead of exploding, he combined his customer's request, his simmering temper, and cooking oil to create something he thought was insane. Muttering under his breath, he sliced the potatoes almost paper thin and fried them until they were hard as a rock. To his surprise the customer loved them and wanted more. Today potato chips are served in restaurants around the world. [11]

Even aggravating people can be part of the puzzle pieces that lead to the creation of a product that millions will want to buy. Keep on putting the pieces together until you come up with a solution. My friend who worked with the energy of water used to say, "Tell me everything." When I complied, sometimes he would sigh because I gave him more information than he wanted. Even so, he loaded those details into his brain, spun them around, and every once in a while he came up with intriguing conclusions.

When you use this tool, never consider any detail too trivial. Those seemingly unimportant pieces could be the key

---

[11] *Ibid*

to developing a compelling new idea, something that could move your business forward in a big way.

SIXTH TOOL - INSPIRATION

The inventor Thomas Edison once said, "Genius is one percent inspiration and ninety-nine percent perspiration." If you have worked with an idea person who generated tons of ideas but had little desire, motivation or skill to turn them into something usable, you have experienced firsthand how true that quote is. Ideas are a dime a dozen. Almost everybody gets them, but not as many people are willing to take the time and effort to bring them to life.

An idea that seemed dynamic when you thought it up can quickly lose its luster when you try to make it work. However, it's during those challenging moments of trying to make it work that inspiration sometimes flashes solutions into your mind. It may happen while you're working on the idea, while you're sleeping, or when you're doing something totally unrelated. It seldom happens if you don't do all you can to try and make it work.

After I volunteered to be in charge of the Easter program for our church one year, I thought about backing out. I didn't want to have a conventional service or write my own Easter play, which I'd done in some past years. I wanted something different, but no ideas came. Finally, I found a play that someone else had written, which might work but wasn't quite what I wanted. Even so, I pondered how to make it work. As I walked from one room to another with the play in my hand, inspiration struck. The idea came full blown like a light bulb turning on above my head, just like in the comics!

What if we had a celebration-of-life Easter service in which members of the congregation pretended to be people in the

Bible who had crossed paths with Jesus, people like the blind beggar, one of the apostles, a member of Jesus' family, Mary Magdalene, Lazarus, and Zacchaeus? In their own words, they could talk about how Jesus affected their lives. And so was born one of the most unusual and meaningful Easter services our church has ever had. It wouldn't have happened if I hadn't kept trying to come up with an idea when nothing seemed to work.

Inspiration operates that way. It comes when we least expect it, when nothing seems to gel, when we've done everything we know how to do. It's a tool that reminds us never to give up even when things seem impossible. Inspiration has a way of showing up at the last minute. If I could redesign that tool, I'd make it show up a lot sooner. But maybe inspiration strikes after we've exhausted our mind so it gets quiet enough for us to hear what our heart has to say.

SEVENTH TOOL - MATCHMAKER

This tool came with an image to help me understand its possibilities. I saw what reminded me of a brown, rotating globe that was not tilted. An outer ring circled it, and the ring contained marks that looked like bumps.

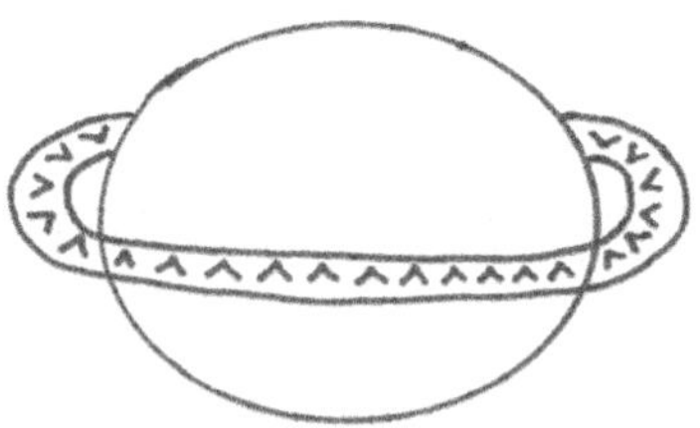

When I asked for more information so I could understand this tool, I was told its purpose is to match people's personalities, strengths and weaknesses with the positions they can handle well. That's a business tool that could have great benefits!

To use this tool, imagine thinking of one specific person. You may want to know what that individual has to offer, what job in the company they will handle well, what committee in an organization on which they might serve well, or what position they should play on a sports team. In your mind, on the globe's outer ring give each bump a designation, such as a particular job, a committee or a team position. If there are only a few jobs, committees or positions to choose from, give several bumps the same designation until every bump on the outer ring represents one of those positions. As you think of the person you have in mind, see that person standing in a particular place on the globe. Then imagine spinning the globe. When the spinning stops, match up the person's place on the globe with the bump on the ring closest to it. On a piece of paper write the person's name and the job, committee or position on which the spin landed. Remember, the globe is just a concept, a tool to help your mind and heart make the best match possible.

Play around with this tool. See how well you can match people with a variety of different possibilities. Businesses function better when employees are well matched with positions that allow them to use their strengths. If you match people with positions that require skills they're not good at, the employees will be unhappy, the company will not benefit, and the mismatched people may decide to quit. Some bosses would say good riddance, but what if those people would have performed magnificently in different positions that highlighted their strengths? If they quit or are fired, everyone loses. With good matchmaking skills, everyone can win.

EIGHTH TOOL - SHIELD

It is important to put a strong shield around yourself and

your business to provide protection against people who may try to send unhealthy energy your way. Those attacks can come from anywhere. Perhaps a shopkeeper having a bad day feels angry because you left the store without buying something. Those angry vibes can cling to your aura, to the energy field around you. Maybe someone was unhappy with a business deal he made with your company. He could send bitter thoughts toward your business, and those thoughts could contaminate the energy field that surrounds your company.

Yes, businesses have energy fields. So do buildings, vehicles, parking lots, and every product you make. Surround yourself and your entire business, including each product, with an energy shield of protection.

Here's one way to do it. Sit quietly in a place where you will not be interrupted. Meditate and pray until you feel like you're in the present moment. Thank God for helping you form this shield and ask that it will have great strength to protect you.

Make sure you are well grounded. Then imagine a white light moving from the center of your body, slightly below your belly button, and continuing up through your stomach, heart, neck and head until it flows out the top of your head and continues upward into the sky and far beyond it to the center of the universe. Imagine yourself wrapping that light firmly around an unbreakable rod there. As the light wraps itself tightly around that rod, check to make sure that the light's connection with the rod is firm and that nothing can shake it loose.

Then retrace the light down from the center of the universe, back through the top of your head. Follow the light through your body, down your legs, through your feet, and watch it bore deeply into the Earth, where it wraps its light around an anchor at the center of the Earth so securely that nothing can budge it.

Then watch the light move back up your legs and into your power center just below your belly button. Feel both ends of the light, from the Earth and from God, blend together in a firm, unbreakable tie at your power center, which is just below your belly button. See the shield of light expand out from you in every direction until it extends several feet around you. Watch it wrap itself around your business, the building, room or corner in which it operates and all the products and services that your business provides.

Keep watching the light and ask God to make that shield of light so strong that nothing can penetrate it. If someone does try to send something negative your way, say, "Return to sender with love." Your intent is to help the erring attackers waken to the truth of who they are, magnificent children of God, and to remember that you are all One. When that sense of Oneness prevails, you all have the opportunity to make the choice of working together so that everyone can live in the light of God's unconditional love. If any choose not to work together, that is their choice. Remember the strong shield that you formed around yourself and know that it will protect you from any attempt to harm you.

After you have installed this shield, tell yourself every day, "My shield is strong," to remind yourself that it's there. Often thank God for it. Know that you and your business are protected and that this shield will always be with you.

NINTH TOOL - SYNCHRONICITIES

When you focus on something intently, whether it's a project you're working on or a thought that keeps entering your mind, you may discover unexpected connections, opportunities, or people popping up in your life. You might meet someone who has the information you need to complete a project. Perhaps you'll see a sign that contains a word describing exactly what you've been thinking about. You may watch a television show, listen to something on the radio, see a billboard, or take in a movie that deals with the very issue with which you've been grappling.

Those seeming coincidences are called synchronicities. If you are working on a project that captures your imagination and that you think about almost all the time, it's likely that synchronicities will occur.

When I was writing an article for an in-flight magazine about a destination point near where I live, I visited the place, talked with people and business owners about it, and read many pieces of information relating to it. As I immersed myself in the subject, I found all kinds of synchronicities popping up. I drove down a street and noticed the front yard of someone's house had been dedicated to the place I was writing about. I found myself standing next to someone in line at a restaurant who had information I needed for the article. I came across a news release about the destination point with just the information I was looking for. One thing or person after another appeared in my life to help make that article a success.

These synchronicities are important for you as an individual and a business owner or employee. They open windows of opportunity that, if you take them, will enhance your success and shine a light of anticipation on each day. It's fun to discover what or who will turn up next to assist you.

You too can show up as a synchronicity in another person's life. You may have just the skills they need or you might offer the word of encouragement they're seeking. Perhaps you will have the information they need. Synchronicity makes life more exciting and gives you another reason to welcome the new day so you can experience the amazing connections that will occur.

TENTH TOOL - VISION

This tool involves planning ahead and seeing the long-term purpose for your business. Many businesses discuss the company's vision before they write it down in just a few words. That vision becomes a guide to help them follow the company's main purpose, the overall goal it hopes to achieve. It doesn't outline a plan to achieve that goal but states it in such a way that everyone knows the purpose of the business.

Here are a few examples of vision statements:

- Oxfam: A just world without poverty.
- Feeding America: A hunger-free America.
- Habitat for Humanity: A world where everyone has a decent place to live.
- Make-A-Wish: Our vision is that people everywhere will share the power of a wish.
- San Diego Zoo: To become a world leader at connecting people to wildlife and conservation.
- Ducks Unlimited: Wetlands sufficient to fill the skies with waterfowl today, tomorrow and forever.
- Smithsonian: Shaping the future by preserving our heritage, discovering new knowledge, and sharing our resources with the world.
- Community of Christ: We proclaim Jesus Christ and promote communities of joy, hope, love and peace.
- Special Olympics: To transform communities by inspiring people throughout the world to open their minds, accept and include people with intellectual disabilities and thereby anyone who is perceived as

different. [12]

Just as businesses have a vision statement, individuals can have one too. The vision for our purpose may change over time, but if we can articulate what it is at this moment, we can make better decisions about what activities to pursue, who to spend our time with, and what causes to champion. When the decisions we make nurture the integrity of our purpose, we feel happier, more fulfilled and more successful.

---

[12] *topnonprofits.com/examples/vision-statements/*

CHAPTER 7

MARKETING TOOLS

Marketing tools often bring to mind the internet and all the connections available there. They also point to advertising, public speaking, appearing on popular television and radio shows, and many other ways to get the word out about the product or service you may have to sell. It surprised me that the marketing tools presented by the trees had little to do with those methods. Instead, many relate to our emotional health and our attitude toward ourselves, others, and the services or products we are trying to market.

Although traditional marketing tools are important and very useful, the tools presented here provide food for thought about how our attitudes affect the success of our business. If we put more focus on these tools, might we discover that our products and services sell better and reach a larger market?

FIRST TOOL - NICHE

Spend time thinking about and researching your product or service to identify a niche in the market it can fill. Are there pockets of people or types of needs not being adequately served that will benefit from what you have to offer?

During your time of meditation or prayer, think about the product or service you have to offer. Ask, "How may I help?" Listen for the answer. You may be surprised at the ideas that flood your mind.

Spend time researching your product. Check out online marketplaces, local stores, books, magazines, every place you can think of to discover if a product or service such as yours could be used in a unique way to meet needs that are not adequately being addressed.

Streamline your product or service so that it specializes in meeting that unmet need you discovered in your research. Identify needs or wants that competitors are not addressing, and gear your product to satisfy those wants and needs. That's where research will be of special help to you.

Unleash your intuitive skills by seeing if you can recognize something that people don't even realize they want. Market your product or service to meet those unrecognized desires. The late Steve Jobs of Apple Inc. was especially good at figuring out what people didn't know they wanted in the field of electronic gadgetry. Once they saw it advertised, they realized they wanted it very much.

A few examples of niche markets are diesel gas in the area of engine fuels, solar energy as a way to generate electricity, and massage as a specialized way to address health challenges such as muscle cramps.

To help understand what you do best, ask yourself what products or services your clients would have the hardest time replacing if your business closed. Answer that question, and you will grasp the uniqueness of what your company has to offer and what you do best.

Above all, focus on your strengths, what you love to do and where your passions lie. If you love what you do and are skilled at it, you will do it well. Word of mouth will help to spread the news about what you have to offer.

SECOND TOOL - CONFIDENCE

Whatever product or serve you offer, have confidence in it. Believe beyond a shadow of a doubt that it's valuable and that it can help others. If you don't truly believe that, you're doing yourself and others a disservice by promoting it. Often the difference between one person's success and another's failure is their belief in what they have to offer.

If you're not convinced your product or service can make a positive difference in someone's life, you won't sound enthusiastic or believable. You may put on a good show, but people can see through that pretty quickly. The best con artists in the world may be able to fool a lot of people, but energetically they are hurting themselves by being less than honest. That deceptive energy attracts similar energy that can bring about unpleasant consequences. The circumstances may be different, but the energy surrounding those circumstances will have a vibrational frequency similar to the deceptive energy.

Sometimes, though people are confident that their service is good, they're not sure they can do it very well. They lack confidence in themselves. They think they're not good enough. Most of the time, that sense of inadequacy is simply not true. It's a belief their subconscious mind accepted as accurate, and that belief influences everything they do and think. Each of us has a great deal to offer, and we offer it in our own unique way. If we can let go of the false beliefs that limit us, we will have a much better chance of realizing success.

To help bolster your belief in your product or the way in which you provide a service, ask people if they would be willing to write a brief statement about how that product or service benefited them. Get their permission to use the statement on your website, in your brochures, and in any other marketing that you do. When a chiropractor put together his own website, including a page of statements from grateful clients, those kind words made his heart sing. They reminded him of the positive effect he was having in the lives of his patients. He was already confident about his abilities, but the words raised his spirits. We all can benefit from having our confidence boosted, especially on difficult days.

THIRD TOOL - KNOW YOURSELF

Know who you are. That's easy to say, but it's often hard to accomplish. Other people may know us better than we know ourselves. All too often we overlook our strengths and concentrate on our weaknesses. We emphasize the mistakes we make and the inadequacies we feel. It's important to recognize both what we do well and what we don't do so well. Focus on what you're good at and let others handle everything else.

Less usual are the people who think they have all the answers, who don't recognize their shortcomings. They surround themselves with "yes" people who say only good things about them and their ideas because they're afraid of being punished or belittled. Be open to suggestions, to ideas that may not reinforce yours. Don't think of it as someone criticizing you. Think of it as people wanting to help make you and your business even better.

You are a unique person with important and valuable talents and skills, and those skills and talents are what you should be marketing. Keep reminding yourself of your abilities. If there are contests in your area of expertise, enter some of them to see how you stack up against other people in your field. You'll likely discover that you do pretty well, and people who judge your work may suggest how you can perform even better. Use those suggestions to hone your skills.

Don't be afraid to look at your shadow side, where you've stored things you don't want to see in yourself. You may have some amazing abilities that you've hidden away because when you used them before, somebody made fun of you or hurt you in some way. As a result, you learned to hide those parts of yourself, and perhaps you even came to fear them. In some cases, you may need the help of a professional counselor or psychotherapist to explore those hidden treasures and reintegrate them into the wholeness of who you really are. Don't be afraid to ask for help when you need it.

When you truly know yourself, you will feel confident about marketing the talents and skills you have to offer. And you'll be of even greater service to others.

FOURTH TOOL - RESPECT OTHERS

Once you know yourself well and have dealt with your own issues, it is easier for you to respect others and see their potential. Recognize that they have wisdom and valuable information to offer. When you respect others, you are respecting yourself, for we really are all One. When you disrespect others, make fun of them, gossip about them behind their backs, or harbor unkind thoughts about them, you are finding fault with yourself as well.

It's a truth that you can't get around no matter how much you might disbelieve it. When you show respect and love for others, you are showing it to yourself as well. It's good business to have a positive attitude about everyone, including yourself. When you have that kind of attitude, you're more pleasant to be around. It will likely attract new customers and clients to you.

When you honor and respect other people, they feel better about themselves, and they're likely to treat the next person they meet better too. By lifting the spirits of one person, you make them feel better. Then it's more likely they will treat the next person they meet with greater respect and compassion.

That makes the Respect Others tool a potent instrument for bringing about good will and spreading peace around the globe.

FIFTH TOOL - STILLNESS

At first I couldn't figure out what the fifth tool was. I tried to understand what the Power Tree had to tell me, but nothing came to mind. As I stood quietly, keeping my mind open, I saw a deer lying in the pasture beyond the tree. It lay perfectly still as it observed me. After a few moments, it ambled into the bushes. I felt peaceful in the stillness of that moment.

That's the fifth tool: Stillness. Be quiet, be still, and observe. Don't try to pray, solve problems, plan or think about anything at all. In the stillness you become aware of things you might not have recognized otherwise. Ideas that can benefit your business will come during those moments of quiet. Unique ways to market your product will pop into your mind when you take the time to be still.

In his blog, *The Practice of Stillness,* best-selling author Michael Hyatt wrote about how doing nothing means simply to be. He quoted Mother Teresa, who has been made a saint by the Catholic Church. She expressed the importance of stillness this way. "We need to find God, and He cannot be found in noise and restlessness. God is the friend of silence. See how nature - trees, flowers grass - grows in silence; see the stars, the moon and the sun, how they move in silence. ... We need silence to be able to touch souls."[13]

When we touch souls, we do our best marketing. The stillness we create carries a peacefulness that provides an oasis of calm. It touches and heals other people even though they

---

[13] *michaelhyatt.com/the-practice-of-stillness.html*

may not recognize what's happening. They just know they feel better when they're around us or in the vicinity of our business, and so they come more often. In that way, the stillness tool becomes an effective marketing strategy.

SIXTH TOOL - RECOGNIZE THE DIVINITY OF OTHERS

The Power Tree felt so powerful on the day it taught me the sixth tool. It made me feel more powerful too, and I knew this tool would be especially important.

We are all divine beings. As *A Course in Miracles* says, you are God's holy children, "forever innocent, forever loving and forever loved, as limitless as your Creator, and completely changeless and forever pure."[14]

We are limitless, powerful beings, and when we recognize that truth in another person, we recognize it in ourselves. This acknowledgement helps us all to heal and to become aware of how awesome we really are.

What does a tool like this have to do with marketing? When we recognize who we are, we take a step toward healing and wholeness. When we recognize the value in others, we validate them in a way that lets them truly hear what we have to say. They can hear us because they feel more whole, less corroded with false beliefs about themselves. If what we have to market helps them feel better about themselves, they are more likely to respond to it.

Sometimes it's hard to recognize the divinity in others because something has happened that sets us on edge. When those jagged emotions make it hard for us to see our own divinity, let alone the divinity of someone else, try this

---

[14] *A Course in Miracles, Workbook for Students,*"What Is the Last Judgment?", p. 455, *The Foundation for Inner Peace,* Mill Valley, CA, 1975

exercise. Deconstruct the energy around the word or phrase that captures what robbed you of your peace of mind. Some examples might be "people who are always late," "disrespect," "cyber-crime," "dishonesty," "complainers," "I can't do anything right," "I don't feel safe," "I'm not good enough," "backseat drivers," "control freaks," "incompetent bosses," "uncooperative employees," "fickle friends," or "fear of failure."

To begin this exercise, either sit in a chair or on the floor. Focus on your root chakra, which is located where your legs meet your body. Then say in your mind the word or phrase you have chosen. Let your body move any way it needs to move so it can express that feeling. At this point, some people go into a fetal position representing fear or a sense of victimhood. Others act out different feelings. They may express them in movement, sound or in some other manner. Let your body move any way it needs to. Keep focusing on your root chakra until you feel ready for the next step.

When you're ready, move up to your abdomen and focus again on the word or phrase. From this position, your body may react differently than it did when you were at the root chakra. Think of yourself as a jaguar in the jungle, constantly alert to everything around it. Survey your surroundings on both a physical and nonphysical level. What do you see or sense that may give you more insight into the word or phrase you have chosen? Give your body time to react to your experience at this abdominal level. Let your body move in any way it needs to. Body movement can help you work through whatever you need to let go of.

Move up to your third eye in your forehead. Again, think about the word or phrase. Say it out loud if that will help you. Pay attention to how your body reacts to it. While you stay in your third eye, look at the bigger picture. You may arrive at a more peaceful understanding of what the word or phrase would like to teach you.

Once you feel you are ready, imagine that all the negative energy the word or phrase carries for you begins to release through the top of your head, up and away from you. People often feel lighter and more peaceful after they take time to do this exercise. Try it anytime you feel overwhelmed because of something that happened or you are at your wit's end because of a feeling that won't go away. Sometimes you have no idea why that feeling persists. This exercise may give you more clarity or simply release the energy that seemed to root the feeling in place.

Doing this exercise may not seem related to marketing. But it is. The more clear and peaceful you can be about yourself, the more likely you will be able to discern the divinity in others. When you can do that, your potential customers will sense that you're more comfortable with yourself and with them. As a result, people will be more receptive to you and to the product and service you have to offer.

SEVENTH TOOL - LET GO

This tool is all about letting go of what you no longer need. Don't hang onto old attitudes, old business concepts, old ideas about who you are that no longer serve you. Let them go. Shed them like a snake sheds its skin.

The more cluttered you become with business plans and goals that no longer match the vision of who you and your business are, the less effective you and your business will be. You can't market yourself well when you're operating on a set of false or outdated premises. Let go of what no longer suits you, and focus on what does serve you well.

On the other hand, never forget what makes you unique and what brought you success in the first place. You may have to narrow the focus of what you offer if your business grows so much that you can't provide everything you once did. The more you try to become all things to all people, the less effective you will be. Change when the need calls for it so that you can offer clients your unique services in the best and most effective way possible.

As you meet with people in your business or organization to discuss what service or products to emphasize, pay special attention to what capabilities each person has to offer. When you match those capabilities with your clients' needs, you offer your customers the most value. Allow people in your organization to shine so that their strong points strengthen your business. They will likely attract customers to your business and become your strongest selling point. Brainstorm new ways to build on your strengths and the strengths of your staff members so you can offer services and products of the highest value to your customers. Let go of those offerings that no longer provide your clients the best service possible.

That weeding out task is similar to what journalists and novelists face. The most beautifully phrased sentences, the ones they love the best, may have to be cut because they don't serve the main purpose. No matter how magnificent a service or product seems to you, if it's not providing the best value to your customer, let it go.

Change can be hard. Familiar routines feel safe and comfortable, but if they no longer serve you well, don't hang onto them. They will drag your business down, and your customers may look for better value elsewhere.

EIGHTH TOOL - GROW SPIRITUALLY

Though the topic of spirituality may seem out of place in the business world, it is becoming a more important component of many businesses. According to Corinne McLaughlin, executive director of the Center for Visionary Leadership, "Spiritual values embraced in a business context include integrity, honesty, accountability, quality, cooperation, service, intuition, trustworthiness, respect, justice, and service."[15]

Research shows that when ethical and spiritual values are brought into the workplace, they bring with them increased profitability, productivity, employee retention, customer loyalty, and brand reputation. Focusing on those values feeds the hunger that some people have to practice their spirituality in the workplace without offending fellow workers.

Many major corporations now hold meditation classes for those who wish to participate. Pete Carroll, coach of the Seattle Seahawks, who won the Super Bowl against the Denver Broncos 43-8 on Feb. 2, 2014, introduced meditation to players who want to participate.

Left tackle Russell Okung is among several players who chose to be part of the meditation practice. "It's about quieting your mind and getting into certain states where everything outside of you doesn't matter in that moment," he said. "There are so many things telling you that you can't do something, but you take those thoughts captive, take power over them, and change them." Meditation is the first step in Carroll's plans to encourage good nutrition and sleep habits, put focus on accountability and optimism, and encourage a supportive atmosphere that lets players seek help for depression, loss, challenges at home, and other issues that can have an effect on

---

[15] *visionarylead.org/articles/spbus.htm*

an athlete's state of mind.[16]

Giving people a chance to practice daily walking in the presence of God, Spirit, Source, or whatever you feel comfortable calling divinity is good for business. When you start each day acknowledging your connection to God, you open yourself to divine guidance that makes a positive difference in everything you do that day, whether you're at work or involved in another activity.

NINTH TOOL - CARRY ONLY WHAT IS YOURS

When I first tried to understand what this tool was, I saw a picture in my mind of tire tracks moving horizontally over my heart. My heart felt heavy, as though someone had driven a huge vehicle over me, leaving tread marks. The tread marks weren't mine. They belonged to someone else, but I had taken on the negative, or heavy, energy as though it were my own.

If we can identify whose energy we are carrying, it's easier to let it go. Take a few seconds to quiet your mind and make a choice to let go of whatever you shouldered for someone else. Maybe they felt disappointed, angry, worried, guilty, or overwhelmed. You can feel compassion for them and even offer to help, but don't carry their heavy energy for them. It's not yours to carry. Let it go. You won't do a good job of marketing if you carry other people's junk.

One way of doing that is to create a ritual after you leave someone's presence or walk out of a store or other building in which you encounter people. Say to yourself, "I cut the cords between me and ___ with unconditional love, unconditional forgiveness and unconditional compassion." You can say the

---

[16]*goodtherapy.org/blog/meditation-visualization-and-respect-secrets-of-seahawk-success-020314*

name of the person you were with or use a broader designation such as "all the people in the store I just left." See yourself slicing through those cords with an imaginary knife. Ask Archangel Michael to help you cut those cords.

When you can't identify whose energy you have taken on, the task of letting it go can be harder. Take time to pray about the situation until you feel the weight fall away. If that doesn't work, seek help from a counselor or someone else you trust. Should that not work, seek the services of a shaman or other healer who is adept at removing negative energies.

At the end of each day take inventory of yourself. If you feel weighed down, track from the moment you got out of bed to find when you first felt a sense of heaviness like tread marks on your heart. When you identify each thing that happened, let each one go one at a time. Often just recognizing what caused the heavy feeling is enough to help you release it. Once you identify the cause, it often seems more manageable and you begin to feel lighter.

Let go of anything that doesn't belong to you. It's easier to do if you clean yourself off every day. The longer you wait, the harder it is to recall when you took on someone else's stuff. If the heavy energy is yours, take time to work through it. Many techniques can help including the three that follow.

Gary Craig's EFT (Emotional Freedom Technique) is a tapping technique that stimulates acupuncture points on the body. The tapping helps to remove blockages in the meridian system, which carries energy through the body. When your body's energy system is disrupted, negative emotions result. They can often be released with this simple tapping method. The tapping points are located on the face, chest, and hands. To learn more about the technique, go to *www.emofree.com*. There are free directions on that site and many helpful videos and examples of how people used EFT successfully in different situations.

Ho'oponopono is a method that allows you to release emotions that make you perform less than at your best or that make you feel inadequate, angry, abandoned, guilty or confused. While focusing on your negative reaction to someone or something, repeat the phrases, "I'm sorry, please forgive me, thank you, I love you." The order in which you say the phrases is not important. You may feel a shift in yourself after you have done this for a while, because you are erasing from your subconscious mind false beliefs that no longer serve you. You might discover that people around you are positively affected as well. As you clear false beliefs from your subconscious, you make it easier for others to shed their false beliefs as well. To learn more about this technique, read *Zero Limits* by Joe Vitale or go to *hooponopono.org*.

Access Consciousness offers pragmatic tools to change things in your life that you haven't been able to change until now. It involves using a series of statements tailored to the situation you face. It is most helpful when used with someone trained in this technique. It taps into your subconscious mind and helps you to release mental barriers and attitudes that do not serve you well. They may have begun in this lifetime, another lifetime, or a different dimension. To learn more, visit *accessconsciousness.com*.

TENTH TOOL - ASSESS CHALLENGES

When you're faced with a challenge, study all aspects of it carefully. Imagine a professional golfer crouching down to examine the terrain the ball must travel. The golfer studies every dip in the ground, every clump of grass, every rock between the ball and the cup. In a similar way, a hiker scrutinizes a trail to identify pitfalls and determine what climbing equipment may be needed.

Marketing creates its own set of challenges. When and how often do you market a product or service? What techniques do you use? How do you avoid the pitfalls of ineffective marketing? How can you appeal to your potential client? How do you make your product or service stand out from everyone else's? What advertising vehicle do you use - television, newspaper, magazine, radio, Internet, mailings, etc.?

Though these questions face people in business, marketing can be used in other aspects of your life as well. We market ourselves based on the way we conduct ourselves. Sometimes we don't even realize we're doing it. Do we do what we say we'll do? Do we treat other people fairly? Do we pretend to be considerate, then kick the dog or cat when we get upset? Do we take care of our tools by putting them away after each use and keeping them clean? Do we have a positive attitude, or do we spend our time complaining? Do we show up on time? Do we keep our deadlines, honor our commitments, and do our fair share? If we make a mistake, do we apologize and make it right?

Every day you will face a variety of challenges in many areas of your life, some of them simple, others more complicated. Think about each task. Ask yourself what it will take to successfully accomplish it. Will you need the help of another person or certain kinds of equipment? What roadblocks must be removed before you can begin the task? Is your goal realistic or based on wishful thinking? Should you do it now or wait until a more opportune time? If you put off the task, what consequences could you face? If you work with certain individuals, what strengths and weaknesses do they have that could benefit or damage your efforts? In what geographic location should you establish your business to be most effective? Can you work from home, or do you need an office somewhere else?

Assessing challenges well will help you become more successful in any endeavor, whether it's business or personal.

CHAPTER 8

RESTING TOOLS

When you want to feel calm, rested and renewed, resting tools will help you find the peaceful harmony and revitalized energy that you seek. They are simple tools. Some we've heard about all our lives. Others we already practice when we grab a few minutes for ourselves.

These tools point the way to peaceful renewal that gives us strength to carry on. Some of them rely on nature to help us find a restful feeling within ourselves. Others call for us to change our attitudes, to trust, or to become physically active.

Some tools may work better for you than they do for others. Experiment to find the ones that give you the most restful results and that you enjoy doing.

FIRST TOOL - LISTEN TO NATURE

Spend time in nature. Stroll down a tree lined path, glide through an emerald green meadow, and sit beside a tumbling stream. Feel your connection with everything around you.

Notice every part of your body, from your feet to the top of your head, as you feel yourself relax.

Hike up a mountain trail. Notice the flowers, the rocks and the trees along the way. Smell their aroma. Touch the solid firmness of a boulder. Notice the nicks in it and the moss growing on it. Let go of stress and worry as you immerse yourself in the fascinating details of nature.

I once wrote an article about a woman in her late 80s who was still climbing 13,000- and 14,000-foot mountain peaks. At an age when most other people retire and take it easy, she had climbed fourteeners 24 times and was making plans to climb more. After her sister underwent cancer surgery, she climbed 14,003-foot Huron Peak near Buena Vista, Colorado. Though frost had already chilled the mountain, on the way back down she spotted a short-stocked, yellow alpine sunflower blooming bright and strong in spite of the cold. She took it as a sign that her sister, who loved flowers, was safe in God's hands no matter what happened. When her sister died, the memory of that yellow blossom thriving in the frosty chill gave her comfort.

A college director of orchestral music also loves to sail. Being part of a sailboat crew on the ocean or a lake helps him let go of stress and feel recharged. Though he's often active on that sailboat, being away from the demands of the job he loves relaxes and renews him.

"Sailing really connects with musicians because it's a visceral experience," he said. "With music, our whole body is affected. As a conductor, I find it's a lot like dancing. The experience of sailing and the wind literally picking you up and moving you down the lake or down the ocean is very much the same."

I am fortunate to live near a river. One of the most restful activities for me is to stand by that river, listen to the water chatter around rocks, and watch geese bounce along as they ride the waves. As I watch and listen, everything else fades from my mind. The sounds of the water lapping against boulders and swishing among weeds on the edge of the bank create such a calming, tranquil atmosphere that visiting the river is like a vital tune-up. It helps me not only survive, but thrive.

Spend time among trees. Acknowledge their beauty,

strength, and usefulness. Listen and absorb what they have to offer you. This exercise can renew your energy and uplift your spirit.

Whatever way you enjoy connecting with nature, take the time to do it as often as you can. It will help you feel relaxed and rested so you can be more productive in whatever activity you pursue throughout your day.

SECOND TOOL - PRAY FOR OTHERS

Make it a habit to pray for others when you sense they need it. If you're walking down a grocery store aisle and spot a harried mother with a child or two in tow, send a silent prayer her way to lift her spirits and give her the wisdom and energy to carry on her important task of mothering those children.

If you're driving on the highway and encounter a distracted driver, say a prayer asking that the driver be alert and focused and experience relief from whatever problems caused the distraction. You not only help yourself, but you improve the safety of everyone else on the road.

When you take a stroll through nature, say a prayer for the trees, bushes, flowers, rocks and rivers or streams by which you walk. They have needs too. Once you establish yourself among the elements of nature as someone who cares, you may feel a tree or a bush calling out to you, asking for prayer. Nature responds to prayer so quickly. Say a prayer, and in the blink of an eye the tree, bush or river absorbs its positive energy.

When you pray for others, you benefit as well. Some part of you, whether you recognize it or not, responds to your prayer for someone else and helps you to feel stronger and more refreshed. Rest in the knowledge, whether you see results or not, that prayer is a powerful tool and that you can use it as often as you like with confidence. If you need a reminder of how powerful prayer is, spend a little time with a tree. When you feel connected with it, say a prayer for its wellbeing. You may feel the tree instantly receive the positive effects of your prayer.

When you attend a meeting, visit a friend in the hospital, or enter your workplace, breathe a silent prayer asking for peace, harmony, wisdom and healing to permeate every activity and every person. Then watch how much more productive, fulfilling and effective the activities become in which you're involved.

THIRD TOOL - STARE INTO SPACE

Look into the distance without thinking about what you are looking at. If you notice what's there, don't dwell on it. Adjust your eyesight so the thing you're seeing is slightly out of focus. Let go of all other thoughts. Simply stare into space. Notice how your mind stops churning and you begin to relax as you let go of all the troubles, anxiety, guilt, or sadness that has weighed you down.

Magic Eye images, which became popular in the 1990s, help you to stare into space and have fun at the same time. A Magic Eye image looks like random splashes of color with repeated patterns, but there's a deeper level to the picture, a lovely image to discover when you learn to look at the picture just right. You can see the three-dimensional picture hidden in the first picture without using any special kind of equipment. But you do have to train your eyes to see in a new way, which includes using more of your peripheral vision than normal. To do it, soften your gaze so the hidden image can appear.

When you're ready to find the hidden picture in a Magic Eye image, breathe deeply and keep on breathing deeply enough to take in plenty of oxygen. Too often when we face a difficult task, we stop breathing momentarily or breathe only in a shallow way. Take deep breaths. Oxygenate your brain. It will help you relax and think more clearly.

Remember to blink. It soothes, moisturizes and relaxes your eyes. Try to enjoy yourself as you look for the hidden image so that you don't tense up with effort. You can reduce tension by smiling, not only with your mouth but with your eyes. Feel your whole body relax when you smile.

Then hold the Magic Eye image right up to your nose. It will be blurry when you look at it. Focus as though you're looking into the distance. Then slowly move the image away from your face until you begin to see depth in the picture. Hold the page still, and the hidden picture will start to take shape. If you find another way that works well for you, use it as long as it helps you to relax.[17]

You probably will notice that as you focus on finding the hidden picture, you have stepped into the present moment where all distress about the past and worries about the future are gone. You are so focused on what is happening right now that you're only aware of this moment. It is a powerful place to be, free from distractions. Staring into space, whether you look into the distance without focusing on anything or whether you use an aide such as the Magic Eye, will help you to feel rested, relaxed and renewed.

FOURTH TOOL - LET GO OF ALL JUDGMENT

If you've ever been upset with someone, you may remember how much energy it took.

---

[17] *Magic Eye Beyond 3D Improve Your Vision, Reduce Computer Eye Strain, Stress & More* by Magic Eye Inc. & Marc Grossman, O.D., L.A.c, Andrews McMeel Publishing, Kansas City, MO, 2004, pp. 5-7.

Your whole body may have felt consumed with anger, frustration, betrayal or desire for revenge. You were so consumed with judging the other person that you couldn't concentrate well on anything else. That's not a peaceful place to be.

Because of the way we've been raised, the experiences we've had, the belief systems of people around us, we've developed attitudes about many things. We've been programmed with beliefs that may or may not serve us well. We've often been trained from an early age to judge and criticize others for making mistakes or for behaving in a way we consider inappropriate. Maybe we adopted an attitude about ourselves based on what we heard other people say about us. In a fit of temper, someone close to us might have said, "You never get anything right," "You're no good," "I wish you were never born," "Girls aren't good at math," "Boys aren't supposed to cry," or "You're a loser."

Our subconscious mind, which has no filter to strain out untruths, accepts everything we're told as true. We see everything through that tarnished filter. It isn't until we start shedding that programming, letting go of those old, erroneous judgments that we can see ourselves and others more clearly.

When we stop judging, we free up energy to focus on doing what we want to do, thinking about what could lead to important discoveries, or experiencing joy. We're no longer covered with the muck of our misconceptions. When we see ourselves through the eyes of unconditional love, we see others that way too. The longer we stay in that loving frame of mind, the lighter we'll feel, as though we've let go of a backpack full of junk that we no longer need.

Try making it through an hour without thinking one judgmental thought. It may be hard at first, but the more you do it the more you'll like the way you feel and the better you'll get at being judgment-free for longer stretches until it becomes a healthy habit.

When we let go of judgment, we begin to remember who we really are. *A Course in Miracles* says, "You are One Self, united with your Creator, at one with every aspect of creation, and limitless in power and in peace."[18]

If we can remember who we are, we will be less likely to judge anyone because we are all cut from the same cloth, we're all part of the whole. If we judge someone else, we're judging ourselves. While I grappled with this concept of judgment and how unhealthy it is for us, I walked across rocks by the side of a river. Each rock had its own size, color, shape, place and purpose on that riverbank. Each was of exquisite value to God. I realized with a rush how crazy it would be to try and criticize any of those rocks. Just as those rocks were equally valued and loved by God, so are each of us. God loves all of nature, including rocks - and us.

It's senseless to judge or criticize each other. If we can focus on realizing that God loves all of us unconditionally and that he has a purpose for each one of us, then we can let go of the habit of judging others for their idiosyncrasies, physical appearance, strengths, weaknesses and the way they push our buttons. Then we can get on with the greater, more fulfilling task of carrying out the purpose for which we came to this planet.

FIFTH TOOL - NOTICE ONE TINY DETAIL

When I was first introduced to this tool, I was standing near

---

[18] *A Course in Miracles, Workbook for Students,* Lesson 95, Foundation for Inner Peace, Mill Valley, CA, 1975, *Workbook for Students,* Lesson 95, p. 167

the Power Tree, struggling to understand what the tool was and how it worked. My gaze locked onto a piece of bark on the cottonwood's trunk that formed a sharp, narrow strip. The more I looked at the sharp narrowness of it, the more focused my concentration became. I found myself in a deep state of meditation without even trying to get there. It was a very restful place to be.

Focusing on one tiny detail doesn't mean trying to pigeon hole it or categorize it. It just means noticing it. Take in every contour, every bump and nuance of color. Notice nothing else. That's when you'll sink into a peaceful state of meditation that helps you to feel rested and recharged so you can tackle whatever the rest of the day or night has in store for you.

Do you feel exhausted or overwhelmed? Focus on an image that has great meaning for you, something that can give you strength and encouragement. It may be an image from your spiritual background or your family history. It could be something in nature or a meaningful gift from someone special.

When Tibetan monks came to a nearby community college, they spent time creating a precise, detailed picture using different colors of sand. I was among many people who gathered around them to watch their progress. I found myself so focused on every tiny detail they were creating that time disappeared. I forgot everything else. When I moved back to let someone else watch, I felt relaxed, peaceful and calm, almost as though I'd taken a refreshing nap.

That's what happens when you focus on one tiny detail. You give your mind a rest from its constant chatter, and you think only about the detail you are noticing.

SIXTH TOOL - ACCEPT THE LOVE OTHERS SEND YOU

It's often hard for us to love ourselves. Accepting the love others offer us can be even harder. We might be in a relationship in which we never let ourselves be truly loved by our partner. The physical relationship may be excellent, but the spiritual one is weak because we can't believe we're worthy of love. We're convinced another person wouldn't love us if they really knew us with all our rough edges exposed.

We're our own worst critic. We see our defects in stark detail. As a result, we often can't accept love from others. We think we don't deserve it, that we're not lovable. If someone tells us they love us, we don't believe them or we wonder what strings are attached. Do they want something in return? Will they be vindictive if we don't give them what they want? As we wallow in fear or anxiety, we churn ourselves into a state of exhaustion. We cut ourselves off from the people who care most about us.

Instead of trying to evaluate another person's motives for loving you or wanting to help you, recognize the other person's worth. Remember that deep down they are part of who you are, they are One with All that Is. They have within themselves a piece of divinity just as you do.

Open your heart to the love that flows from God to you through a person, animal, or tree. Let yourself feel guided by that love. Know that when you accept the love others send, you are accepting love from All that Is. Allow that love into your heart, expanding it until it engulfs your entire body, fills your aura and extends to its outer edges. When you are so filled with the light of God's unconditional love, you are safely surrounded by the strongest, most powerful energy in existence. Absorb the power of that love. Let it permeate every cell in your body.

Accepting the love others send you does not mean you have to give up control of your life or open yourself to a relationship you don't want. It means that you are willing to recognize the divine nature that's deep within that person, the same nature that is part of you. Accept that love. Send your own in return. It will help you both feel stronger, healthier and more whole. Such genuine love has no strings attached, no demand for anything in return.

There is nothing more relaxing and strengthening than to accept unconditional love, knowing there are no attachments, no restrictions, no requirements, no qualifications. Allow yourself to recognize that you are worthy of receiving love from every being of Light in this universe who is willing to send it to you. Receive it with gratitude and send your own in return. In that way, we remind each other of how worthy we all are to be loved no matter what.

SEVENTH TOOL – TRUST THE GUIDES IN YOUR LIFE

You have so much divine guidance around you all the time. God is always ready to help you if you request that help and listen to it. Your guides operate in God's unconditional love. They include angels, archangels, spirit guides, power animals, and others who have your best interests at heart. From the time you chose to come into this life they have been assisting you.

They are always there to help you, but you must tell them you want their help. They will never violate your right to make your own choices and follow your own path, even if it's one they know will not be good for you. Once they know you welcome their help, expect them to be involved all the time. I have some loyal, loving trees who frequently help me. Their spirits sometimes travel with me. They go to healing sessions with me, both when I am helping others and when other healers are working to help me. They have sometimes suggested using techniques that I'd never heard of before but that were exactly what was needed in the moment.

More than anything, they are present to lend their support and their love.Your guides tell you the truth. They will never steer you wrong. You may feel surrounded by infinite love when they are around. If you feel heavy, uncomfortable and unable to think straight, it's possible that negative energies or your own misdirected thoughts are annoying you or trying to lead you off of your path, away from the purpose for which you came into this life. If you sense that and can't get rid of it, take some shamanic classes or get a treatment from someone who knows how to remove negative energies.

You will be most creative, productive and happy when you're not bothered by negative or heavy energy and when you are fulfilling the purpose for which you came into this life. Your guides are good at helping you find ways to stay focused on your chosen pathway so that you experience joy, delight, and a sense of fulfillment.

EIGHTH TOOL - EXERCISE

Exercise helps to stretch and strengthen your muscles, improve your bone health, bolster your immune system, lower your cholesterol, and stimulate your mind partly because more oxygen is circulating through your body. It has many other benefits as well.

Exercising helps you find peace, harmony, balance and greater health. It helps you to be better grounded, and it stimulates the meridian system that directs the flow of energy through your body. Those meridian pathways bring energy to your organs. When those pathways are blocked, you may feel sluggish or lethargic or not able to think clearly. Exercise helps to clear and balance those pathways so every area of your body gets what it needs to function well.

While you exercise, take a few seconds to thank your body for all it does for you. Moving your body in a state of gratitude and awareness can take you to a higher energy vibrational level. Everything is made up of energy, even you and me. That energy within each of us vibrates at certain levels. At the lowest levels, we are more consumed with self-preservation, anger, guilt, depression and other negative emotions. At higher vibrational levels we function at varying degrees of love, peace, harmony and joy. During exercise, you may discover that you feel happier. One reason for that is because your energy is vibrating at a slightly higher level due to the exercise you're doing and the focus you're placing on that activity.

One of the best exercise books I've found is *7 Minutes of Magic: The Ultimate Energy Workout* by Lee Holden with Doug Abrams, Avery, NY, 2007. It provides a basic set of exercises drawn from practices such as yoga, qi gong and meditation mixed with a few weight bearing exercises.

For me, the exercises take about an hour, because I've added a few drills of my own. But you can spend only seven minutes with these exercises and gain good benefits.

Holden describes the value of exercising: "Within each of us there is a place that is full of energy, health, and happiness. This is our natural state, but we so often lose touch with it in our busy, distracted lives. A visit to this place of inner vitality and harmony every day, even for a brief seven minutes, allows us to access a higher level of energy, strengthen our immune systems, and transform the patterns and assumptions that limit our bodies and minds."[19]

---

[19] Holden, Lee. *7 Minutes of Magic*. Avery, NY, 2007. p. 4

When you exercise, you become more aware of what your body does for you every day. Thank every part of your body for the way it serves you. Address each part as you exercise it, whether it's your feet, legs, torso, arms or neck. As you dwell in that state of gratitude, you are exercising your mind by helping it to stay in an attitude of thankfulness. It allows good things that vibrate at the level of gratitude and thanks to flow to you and help you feel more rested.

Find a way to exercise every day, even if it's just walking outside, enjoying the fresh air and the nature that surrounds you. That alone will improve your frame of mind and stimulate your muscles.

NINTH TOOL - KNOW YOU ARE NOT ALONE

At an event during which Mother Teresa gave a speech in the United States, people who planned the occasion wanted to raise money for the work she did among the poor. She graciously declined. Instead, she suggested that they go into the city streets, find people in need, and let them know they are not alone. When people feel alone, they feel isolated, separated, hopeless, and desolate. Their spirits sag. They sometimes give up on life, or they turn to violence in a desperate attempt to be noticed or to force a change. They feel anything but rested.

The truth is that we are never alone. We have around us angels, archangels, spirit guides, power animals and other divine helpers who want to assist us. They're rooting for us, and they want us to succeed. I feel blessed beyond measure that several wonderful trees have decided to spend their time helping me. Some of them also visit my friends in spirit and assist them. I'm delighted when friends tell me how the trees have helped them. One friend who visited the Healing Tree several times with me described how the cottonwood came to her when she was miles away from it. She faced a physical and emotional challenge, and the cottonwood arrived to offer help. It has visited her several other times as well when she needed encouragement. Its spirit remains unfettered and can travel anywhere, lending its help. Other friends have told me they've been visited by the Healing Tree in times of need as well.

Angels are among helpers who assist us. They're around us all the time, wanting so much to help but never interfering unless we ask for it. My best friend, who is sensitive to many things in the environment, lives in a mobile home park. Across the street from her lived a middle aged man with several addictions. He coped with the challenges in his life by playing loud music with a strong bass beat. It didn't seem to bother most people, but it rattled my friend to the core. She felt the vibrations as assaults on her body, mind and spirit. After she explained her situation to the man, he turned down his music for a while, but he soon resumed played it as loudly as ever.

She couldn't sleep. She couldn't concentrate. Every beat of the music felt like a blow. Nerve wracked and exhausted, in desperation she prayed, asking her angels for help. They taught her an exercise that brought her huge relief. With their help she learned that peace and quiet live in our breath. No matter what goes on outside of us, we can always find peace and quiet in the breath.

She discovered that when she took a breath and focused on the present moment with the awareness that peace and quiet live in her breath, her awareness of that reality grew and grew until it connected with her own core, where peace and quiet always live. As she continued to focus on the moment and her breath, she felt herself uniting with the eternal peace and quiet within her. Then she felt at rest.

For years she had meditated, breathing in and out, feeling her breath, counting her breaths, noticing her breaths. All that time, she didn't realize that her breath holds the peace and quiet already living inside of her. Angels helped her understand that. Before, when she became distressed physically or mentally, it was difficult to find peace and quiet. Now it's just a breath away. She practices this technique at work, at home, in traffic, and whenever she feels any kind of distress. It calms her nervous system.

"It's a wonderful thought to think that I'm one breath away from peace and quiet," she said. "If I don't have it now, it's in the next breath. It's a matter of where I place my awareness."

The angels assured her they were working on a long-term solution regarding the man and his loud music. Though the loud music continued, the breathing tool gave her peace. It expanded her consciousness, putting her in a calm frame of mind that let her rest in the peace and quiet already within her.

One day she looked out the window and noticed that the man was packing up. He was moving out of the park. She never learned why he moved, but she felt grateful that her helpers had found a way to alleviate the problem. It's easier for her to feel restful now, not only because the noise is gone but because her angelic helpers were with her and found a way to help her cope.

TENTH TOOL - GRATITUDE

Gratitude is one of the most powerful tools we have. It lifts us from the doldrums of worry, anxiety, and micromanaging and brings us to a place of peace. When you feel like you're mired in the daily grind of life and unable to enjoy it or to find rest, thank God for every aspect of the moment, even its most unpleasant parts.

At the end of each day, find something you can be thankful for, whether it was seeing a butterfly light on a flower, watching brightness fill the room when you flipped on the light switch, or sinking your teeth into a fresh, tasty apple. Make a habit of writing down a few things that happened during the day for which you feel grateful. The practice will lift your spirits if you do it every day for a few weeks.

When a client came to see me, concerned that her solar plexus seemed choked with unrest and that she felt stuck and unfulfilled, she experienced some relief during the session. But her energy didn't flow smoothly until toward the end of the treatment one of her spirit guides suggested that she focus on feeling grateful. Once she absorbed that message, all her blocked and sluggish energy released. She called me the next day to report freedom from all the angst that had been plaguing her. When she filled her mind with gratitude, she freed herself.

One of my aunts told me that she woke up each day saying, "This is the day the Lord has made. I will rejoice and be glad in it." That was her way of living in gratitude, and it worked for her. In spite of many challenging events in her life, she found things to be grateful for, and her gratitude helped her to thrive.

If you practice being grateful in your own way every day, you will discover doors opening for you that wouldn't have opened otherwise. They will open because, instead of focusing on things that drag you down, you are being grateful for what brings you joy. In that way, the vibrational frequency of your energy rises and draws to you similar positive experiences. Gratitude is a restful and productive place to be.

CHAPTER 9

SERVICE TOOLS

I used to think that service involved volunteering our time or doing the best job we could at work, play or in our homes. After discovering what the trees had to say about service, I realize it's much more than that. It's also about honoring and acknowledging what others have to offer, taking care of and nurturing our own selves, and keeping our hearts open to the love that others want to give us.

Service is all about appreciating and honoring ourselves and others. It's not something we provide just to other people; we give it to ourselves as well. It's a way of seeing everyone, including ourselves, as worthy of receiving the very best.

FIRST TOOL - ACKNOWLEDGE OTHERS

Acknowledge that other people are worthy, that they have valuable things to offer, and that they have a right to be part of the community, neighborhood or family. Show them respect.

That's not always easy, especially when their habits create problems for others or their personalities clash with yours. Acknowledge their worth anyway. It has been said that the most difficult people in your life are also your greatest teachers. Ask God what they have to teach you. Then be willing to listen and learn.

In a difficult marriage, a friend of mine wondered how long she could put up with the angry, verbally abusive behavior of her husband. Over time, as she grew spiritually and emotionally, she came to a realization.

"He's here to help me," she said one day. A visit to the trees confirmed her growing understanding of his role. The Twinkling Lights/Power Tree told her that in the grand scheme of things, all is well. On a universal level things are unfolding in marvelous, joyous ways. Because she saw only a small portion of the picture, she couldn't see the awesome majesty of what was happening on a much larger scale around her.

As she continued to nurture the relationship with her husband, she saw huge growth in him. Though he sometimes regressed to his old behaviors, those times grew fewer and farther between. When she acknowledged his worth, he changed in positive ways.

It's hard to acknowledge others when they have committed crimes or made mistakes that killed or maimed others. Acknowledge them anyway. Recognize that in the grand scheme of things they have a purpose even if you can't fathom what it is. They may have made choices that derailed their purpose, at least temporarily. They must be responsible for what they've done and accept whatever punishment the judicial system hands down to them.

When you understand there is a greater purpose beyond what you see in the moment, you are more able to let go of judgment. That frees you to forgive so that you're no longer bound by angry, vengeful thoughts. Those negative thoughts could turn you into a bitter person who forgets how to find pleasure and joy in life. Forgiving doesn't downplay what the other person did. It simply releases you from the negative feelings you have harbored.

Acknowledging the worth of others ultimately lets us recognize the worth of ourselves because we are all connected. Hating someone else means we hate a part of who we are.

We'll never find peace until we can acknowledge the value in every single one of us.

SECOND TOOL - ALLOW GOD'S LIGHT TO SHINE IN YOU

There are many ways to use this tool effectively. An easy and gratifying way is to take a deep breath in through your nose and a cleansing breath out through your mouth. Then breathe in again as you imagine love flowing into your heart from every being that wants to send it to you. As it flows in, see it lighting up your heart with the brilliance of God's love. When you breathe out, send your love out to anyone who is willing to receive it. See that love as full of divine light.

Another method is described in *An Ascension Handbook,* channeled material by Serapis.

In that book, Tony Stubbs explains instructions for doing the Invocation to the Unified Chakras. When I practice this exercise, I feel myself filling up with the light of unconditional love. I have rephrased the method here to focus on the light of God's love, but you can read the complete invocation on pp. 125-127 of *An Ascension Handbook.*

Imagine yourself breathing the light of God's love into the center of your heart. See your heart expanding into a beautiful ball of light. Each time you breathe out, express thanks for this divine love. In this way, you let God's light shine in you.

On the next in breath, imagine the light of God's love expanding from your heart into your solar plexus and throat chakras. With each successive in breath imagine that love expanding through your heart to the next sets of chakras. They are the brow and the naval chakras, the crown and the root chakras, then the alpha chakra above your head and the omega chakra below your root chakra. Allow the Wave of Metatron to resonate between your alpha and omega chakras. I imagine this wave as light flowing in an infinity pattern linking each one of your chakras with the other.

Continue this process, imagining the light of God's love flowing through your heart to your eighth chakra, your emotional body, which is located from above your head down to your knees. After you have experienced this expansion, let your emotional body merge with your physical body. Use the same process with your ninth chakra, your mental body, from above your head to your ankles, and your tenth chakra, your spiritual body, occupying a space even higher above your head to even farther below your feet.

Continue breathing in the light of God's love through your heart and expanding it to your 11th chakra, which is your higher self; your 12th chakra, which is True Christ Consciousness, embodying the unconditional love of all ascended masters; your 13th chakra, which is I Am presence, and your 14th chakra, which is Source energy. After expanding into each of those chakras, which are successively higher above your head and farther below your feet, allow each of them to merge with your physical body. After the exercise, imagine that you are completely filled with the light of God's love.[20]

You may find that it's easier to pray or meditate after you've completed this exercise. It moves you a step closer to wholeness and helps you to vibrate at a higher frequency level, where you can more easily feel love, compassion, and pure joy.

THIRD TOOL – RECOGNITION

Tell other people about the good things you've noticed them doing, and compliment them on their achievements. This

---

[20]Stubbs, Tony. *An Ascension Handbook*, New Leaf, Lithia Springs, Georgia, 1999, pp. 125-127.

is especially effective if you do it in a place where others can hear what you're saying. Did someone offer you excellent service, show great patience, demonstrate remarkable skill? Let them know how much you appreciate what they did.

Send cards of congratulations to people when they have accomplished something special. Writing and sending cards isn't done as often as it used to be now that email, social media and texting are so prominent. Recognition received in those ways is meaningful, but there's something special about receiving a card from someone who took the time to purchase the card, write a note to you and pay for the postage to send it. When you take the time to write someone a note, you're recognizing them and acknowledging that they're important enough for you to spend the extra time and money to recognize what they've done.

There are many others ways to recognize people as well. They range from public announcements of their accomplishments to more elaborate recognition such as naming a building after them or erecting a sign or a statue in their name. Most often, the recognition is less obvious. Sometimes it's praise and appreciation spread by word of mouth. At other times it may simply be kind thoughts people think about someone whose value and contributions they recognize, or it could be prayers of appreciation sent their way.

Keep recognition simple, genuine, and heart felt, and you will offer a wonderful service to others.

FOURTH TOOL - ACCEPTANCE

We all have bad days when we'd like to crawl under the covers and stay there for a while.

Because most of us don't have that luxury, we try to put a smile on our face and go about our day, but we may not succeed very well. We might be irritable and hard to be around, or we could be so unfocused that we don't do a good job. We might even have to put up with someone who's having an even worse day than we are.

Accepting others when they're not at their best is a way we can show them they're valuable even when they're unpleasant to be around. That doesn't mean we have to put up with their behavior, especially if it's abusive. We may have to remove ourselves from it so we don't deplete our own energy by being around that negativity, but we can interact with them later when it's a better time for us and for them. In the meantime, we can reserve judgment and recognize their right to have an off day every once in a while.

When we see beyond their imperfections and offer them acceptance during those difficult times, we can lift their spirits and help them feel loved. Many times we're afraid that if we show our bad side, people will stop loving us. Our acceptance of people in every phase of their behavior is one of the most healing things we can offer. It's also one of the most healing things we can receive from others even though that kind treatment could make us feel a bit ashamed of ourselves when we've been acting like jerks.

Some people make such a habit of being negative and judgmental that they don't recognize they're verbally attacking others. Accepting people does not mean condoning that behavior. It means recognizing there is goodness in them despite their behavior. However, you don't have to continue to put up with their unhealthy display of emotions. If the negative behavior becomes difficult for you to be around, distance yourself from that person for as long as needed to maintain your own emotional health. If people act in such negative ways that others' lives are in danger, you may need to call the police or ask others to help you intervene so no harm is done.

Abraham, a group of highly evolved teachers who communicates through Esther Hicks, speaks often about the Law of Allowing. The Law of Allowing, Abraham explains, is about knowing that you are your own point of attraction. How you feel is everything because it's an indication of the energetic vibration you are offering. All kinds of lovely circumstances, events, and pathways light up when you vibrate at a level that helps you feel joyful and fulfilled. Those pathways won't light up with such good opportunities when you spend time judging others or feeling upset about something they've said or done.

When you recognize the value in others even though you don't like what they're doing, you're accepting the part of God that is within them just as it's within you and in everyone and everything that exists. They're not perfect, and neither are you. If you can accept them as divine creatures who have the potential for developing into amazing beings, you will see them not as what they are at this moment but as what they can potentially be. The power of acceptance will open doors for you and bring joy and delight into your life. Remarkably, as you practice the Law of Allowing, you will encounter fewer and fewer unpleasant people.

FIFTH TOOL - HONOR OTHERS

Honoring others is all about recognizing their value and acknowledging that they have something important to offer. Everyone has at least one thing they can share that you don't know or don't understand as well as they do. Take time to learn about or experience what they have to offer. Are they skilled at something that brings you enjoyment? Are they talented musicians, speakers, healers, painters, magicians, actors, engineers, scientists? Go to their performances or lectures, listen to their music, experience their healing touch, study their work, and view their art. Honor what they have to offer by taking the time to experience it.

It's important for you to get your ego out of the way when you honor others. If you feel the need to inform people that you honored them by experiencing what they had to offer, your ego is at work. You honor people by enjoying what they have to offer without informing them about what you did. Honoring others is about recognizing them, not yourself.

If you can only accept help from others if you see it as a learning experience for them, your ego has made an appearance. People who are used to helping others and can't step out of the provider role may have trouble accepting aid. You can't honor others when your own need to be in charge overshadows your willingness to accept others as equals.

Some people feel that, for whatever reason, they are not worthy to receive help. If they could only remember who they really are, holy children of God, who loves them and sees their perfection, they would not fall into the pit of devaluing themselves. Allowing others to serve you is as much a gift you offer to them as they offer to you.

In every circumstance, let yourself be guided by your intuition and by divine helpers who surround you, constantly ready to assist. It is not always wise for you to accept help from anyone who offers it. Use discretion. When it seems comfortable to you, enjoy the help that others provide. When you honor others, you don't devalue yourself. In recognizing others' strengths and talents, you honor yourself as well. We're all connected, all part of the whole. When we value what others have to offer, we value ourselves as well.

It's not always easy to honor others. Sometimes those who are our greatest teachers are the most difficult people for us to be around. Challenge yourself to find at least one thing they do well, and compliment them on it. Your relationship with them may never be delightful, but it might change for the better if you focus on their positive traits.

Honoring others is a way to be of service to them by valuing who they are and what they have to offer. When you honor others, do it from the heart. Mean what you say, and people will recognize it as genuine. When you provide that kind of service, people respond with gratitude. They feel affirmed and strengthened.

SIXTH TOOL - EXPRESS GRATITUDE TO OTHERS

We're all trying to do our best. We take time to deliver quality work in whatever field in which we work, whether for pay or as volunteers. It's not often that someone takes the time to thank us for a job well done. When someone tells us, "Good job," or writes a thank you note, or, even better, tells our boss what great service we've provided, it makes us glow for weeks to come. We can make others feel that same kind of glow if we express our appreciation for them.

Don't go overboard with your thanks. It can start to sound artificial if you do it too often or with too much enthusiasm. But when you see someone doing a job exceptionally well, take the time to tell them you noticed. It will make their day.

There is power in the essence of words. It doesn't matter what language is used. Words spoken in love and gratitude have a strengthening effect on people, plants and even water. In books that have become classics, among them *The True Power of Water* and *The Hidden Messages in Water,* Masaru Emoto detailed his experiments that showed the powerful effects words have on water. When someone introduced him to a type of water that relieved his foot pain, he became intrigued. He began an in depth study of water, which convinced him that water is influenced by external factors that also affect our mind and body. Just as our spirits can be lifted by listening to magnificent music and depressed by criticism or by hearing other people argue, water also can be affected by positive and negative influences.

To prove to skeptics that the information water takes in changes its quality, Emoto secured the help of researcher Kazuya Ishibashi. After two months of effort, Ishibashi was able to photograph ice crystals. The ice crystals made different formations based on information to which they were exposed. To test his theory, he put water taken from the same source into two glass bottles. On one bottle he taped, "Thank you." On the other bottle he attached the words, "You fool." When he froze the water, the bottle with the "Thank you" label created beautiful crystals, while the one with "You fool," developed only fragments of crystals.[21]

Emoto noted that because humans are made up of about 70 percent water, they too are affected by words. "Since the quality of water improves or deteriorates depending on the information given to it," he stated, "the corollary for humans, who are made up primarily of water, is to take in good information,. When we do, our mind and body can become healthier. Conversely, when we take in negative information, we can get sick."[22]

When you say a heartfelt thank you to others, you are

---

[21] Emoto, Masaru. *The True Power of Water: Healing and Discovering Ourselves*, Beyond Words Publishing, Inc., Hillsboro, Oregon, 2005, pp. 2 and 12.

[22] Ibid. p. 16

helping to give them a more positive outlook. In that way, the water in them takes on a greater glow of health.

SEVENTH TOOL - TAKE CARE OF YOUR OWN NEEDS

It used to be considered selfish to take care of yourself first. Now we understand that if we don't take care of ourselves, we won't have the energy to adequately care for others.

Get a good night's sleep. Take a vacation when you need it. Buy clothes you like that look good on you. Spend time in solitude to mend your spirit. If not done in excess, these things strengthen us so we can be of better service to others.

I enjoy being around people and interacting them, but not for long periods of time. After a while, I must get away by myself for a few hours. If I don't take time to be alone, I become exhausted, crabby and unable to provide good service to anyone, including myself. For me, taking time to be alone is absolutely essential. It's not being selfish. It's my way of recharging my batteries, of taking care of myself, so I can serve others better.

One of the worst things you can do is to deny your own needs because you think someone else won't approve. Why do you elevate them to a position of knowing better than you do what you need? You can seek advice and counsel from wise people, but in the end you must determine what you need and recognize that you become a more productive person when you take that vacation, spend that hour alone, buy that piece of equipment you need, or do whatever you know deep down will rejuvenate your spirit. Most people would approve of you doing what's necessary to keep yourself healthy. Sometimes, however, it's easy to let your imagination convince you that no one will approve of what you need to do. In that way, your thoughts become clouded, and you find it more difficult to take care of your own needs.

Put yourself first so you can be a more effective, productive citizen. There's nothing selfish about that. That's why stewards and stewardesses on airlines tell parents to fasten their own life vests and oxygen masks before putting masks and life vests on their children. You must take care of yourself first so you can take care of others. It's okay to do that. Don't let others shame you into neglecting yourself. Taking care of your own needs first is one of the best ways you can serve and inspire others.

EIGHTH TOOL - ASK YOURSELF, "HOW MAY I BE OF SERVICE TODAY?"

Wake up each day and ask God, "How may I be of service today?" If you can get yourself in that frame of mind, plenty of service opportunities will flow to you. Pick and choose projects with wisdom, discernment, and anticipation that resonate with you. There are thousands of worthy causes and many praise worthy requests for assistance that you will hear about. You can't help them all with the limited resources you have.

A friend pondered how to handle all the requests for assistance that came her way. After giving it considerable thought, she chose three organizations she especially liked. Once she made that decision, she donated to them every month. Now, instead of being spread so thin that her money does little to help anyone, she focuses her resources on those three organizations. It makes her feel like she's doing something worthwhile and that she's making a real difference.

Your money is only one of many ways in which you can be of service. Each day you may encounter people who need a smile, a hug, a listening ear or more concrete assistance. Respond with wisdom so that you don't overwhelm yourself or neglect the people and organizations to which you have already made a commitment.

Some people find they can best be of service when they are part of a group. The group may have resources and connections that you couldn't find anywhere else. This can be a wonderful way to help others. Walk away or temporarily stop your involvement if you feel burned out or compromised. You can't be effective when you feel that way.

Other individuals do better when they find ways to serve on their own. My best friend explained, "What brings me joy is when I can serve people as a lone wolf. Then I don't have to conform to what others in the group need or believe." Working alone gives her the ability to follow divine guidance about when, where, and how to provide assistance.

Finding a pathway to service is not about helping others in the way some people think you should. As you grow, you will naturally find ways of service that bring you joy without a feeling of obligation. When any kind of service takes on a sense of obligation, people are more likely to be exhausted and less likely to feel the joy that service can bring.

Spend each day with the eyes of your heart open to serve. It's a creative and lovely way to pass your time, and it brings joy when you connect with people who are a good match for what you have to offer.

NINTH TOOL - GIVE COMFORT

When people have suffered a loss, been traumatized, or faced an upsetting situation, they will almost always be grateful for a little tender loving care from others. Is someone suffering? Offer them comfort. Send a sympathy note, make a phone call, stop by the person's house. Do they just need to be acknowledged? Tell them something personal and supportive. Contact them every few weeks or more, as needed, to let them know they're not forgotten. That personal contact can be invaluable to people who have suffered a loss.

If they need more help, what services can you suggest that will provide the comfort, relief and assistance necessary? Visit your local chamber of commerce, Salvation Army, United Way, or other organizations that provide support in your community. Learn what's available that will match the needs of people you want to assist. You may discover that, though help is available, it's not exactly what they need. In that case, you might recruit friends to help you find creative ways to meet the person's needs.

Pray for people who have reached out to you. Ask that they feel peace, renewal and hope. Follow divine guidance in what to pray for and what steps, if any, to take. Sometimes giving comfort is as simple as letting people know you're in their corner, that you remember them and their circumstances, and that you care enough to call them on the phone, write them a note or keep in touch with them in some other way.

TENTH TOOL - KEEP YOUR ENERGETIC HEART OPEN

Your energetic heart is a place slightly below and behind the physical heart organ in your chest that pumps blood 24 hours a day through your entire body. Sometimes called your sacred chamber, your energetic heart can expand to a much larger area when you allow it to fill with unconditional love.

In that enlarged condition, your sacred heart can share the energy of love with others as needed, and they can share their love with you as well. This creates a flow among you that fills all of you with more love than you could have on your own. This love can be shared between people, elements in nature and anything that is part of God's creation.

Recently when spring arrived after a relatively warm

winter, I suffered a terrible bout of allergies, the worst I've ever encountered. I could feel my body start to shut down. My heart wasn't getting the energy it needed, and I tired easily. I had little energy to pull myself through each day. When the allergies subsided, it took me a few weeks to feel like myself again. I was irrigating one of our three small fields one afternoon when I felt compelled to go to the Medicine Trees Cluster. Uncertain why the urge was so strong, I obeyed it anyway. As I touched the trunks of the narrow leaf cottonwoods, I felt a surge of energy recharge me. I lingered there and soaked up the much needed energy. I felt revived, stronger, and able to handle all that needed to be done that day. I left the trees feeling so loved. The cottonwoods recharged me by letting God's divine love and healing flow from them to me. In the past, sometimes that cluster of trees needed my help, but on this day they were feeding me.

Trees carry so much love and want to share it with us. When we let ourselves receive what they have to offer, our own energetic heart opens up. We feel recharged, renewed. Everything works better when we let our heart fill with unconditional love.

The next time you feel weak, sad or listless, visit some trees or other elements of nature to which you feel drawn. You'll come away feeling better. When your energetic heart is open, all the systems in your body work better. Then your own light shines brighter, and you will feel more productive and happy.

CHAPTER 10

WORSHIP TOOLS

The idea of worship may stimulate memories of being told to be quiet and quit wiggling when you were a child in a church, synagogue, mosque, shrine, temple, pagoda, or cathedral. But worship tools revealed by the trees are much more expansive and include communing with nature, laughing and being playful. Worshipping is more about your frame of mind and your desire to connect with all that is sacred than it is about where you worship or how you behave when you're there.

These worship tools open up the joy and renewal that the act of worship offers to us. It's about celebrating the divine instead of following a set of rules.

FIRST TOOL - CONNECT WITH THE SPIRIT OF GOD

As I tried to understand the first tool, I looked up into the interlacing branches of four cottonwoods that grow near each other - the Elephant, Eagle, Jane, and Twinkling Light/Power trees. They blended, overlapped, and shared space. Just as the branches of those trees mingle, so are we all interconnected. We strengthen, nurture and help each other. When the awareness of our connection grows, we understand that we are intertwined with divinity on our planet.

We become aware of that connection in many ways. Sometimes it happens when we take the time to pray or meditate. The energy around us lifts, vibrating at a higher frequency so that we can more easily experience joy, peace, and love.

At other times, I have felt drawn to a particular tree, and I sense an infinity symbol, which looks like the figure eight, allowing energy to flow between us. Through that symbol, we share the essence of who we are and what we've learned. In that nurturing, loving relationship, it's easier for me to connect with the spirit of God, which lives in all of us.

Sometimes a kindness shown or a gratitude expressed can remind us of our connection with the divine. After my husband died, many people donated money in his memory. Members of the tiny church I attended decided to use the money to landscape the church in his memory and to remember others in the congregation who had previously crossed over. We worked with a landscaper, who helped to shape our ideas and craft a lovely area. It included a tree circled by colored gravel and the names of people who had died painted on river stones, a bench on which people could sit, and a sign containing the name of our church.

Everything went well until we talked with the city about our sign. Though we were located in a single family residential zone, our church property was considered commercial property. So we needed a licensed contractor to apply for a building permit before the city would let us install our sign. The project couldn't be finished without the sign. Hiring a contractor would have cost more than we could afford.

That's when a local contractor who had no connection with the church offered his help free of charge. I had interviewed him a few years before while writing a couple of magazine articles. When I told him about our situation, he went with me to the city, where he signed the building permit. Our landscaping project was back on track, thanks to a man who believed in helping others when he saw a need.

We felt connected to the divine through the kindness of that contractor. He recognized that we are a community, tied together in so many ways. When we let the spirit of God connect us by lending a helping hand or accepting help from others, unconditional love flows through us and blossoms in ways that we may not have imagined possible.

SECOND TOOL - COMMUNE WITH NATURE

Take a walk among trees, through a garden or along a river. Feel the love that flows through the bushes, flowers, trees and undulating water. Acknowledge them, recognize their value and their connection to the divine. Let go of any sense that you are better than they are or that you are the person in charge and should be able to command them to obey you. That is not the essence of your relationship.

Each element of nature has its own purpose, its own reason for being on the planet at this time. Value each part of nature, respect it for what it has to offer, and see in it that spark of divinity that courses through everyone and everything on our Earth. Recognize how we are all One in a rich and wonderful way and how we benefit each other as we fulfill our own purposes.

If you enjoy painting, set up an easel and paint a tree, a hill, a river or a panorama of nature. Feel the land around you, sense its value, respect and acknowledge it. Communing with nature in this way is a lovely form of worship.

A well-known local artist gave me a gorgeous painting she had created of trees and a hill to thank me for something I had done. I hung the painting in my dining room and loved seeing its gold, green and brown colors bring the wall to life. One day I was going through several newspapers spread out on the dining room table that stood against that wall. Suddenly, I became aware of a huge wave of love flowing to me. It felt so good that I sat there for a moment basking in it. I wondered where it came from. Looking up, my eyes caught the hill in the painting on my dining room wall. That hill gripped my attention. Love poured from the hill to me. How could a painting of a hill hold so much love, I wondered? Somehow, the artist had captured the hill so well that she had painted into it the bond she felt with it and the affection it felt for her. The love she had painted spilled out to me. I knew I'd received an incredible gift. I felt like I was worshipping God in a circle of love.

That sense of worship when you commune with nature may surprise you. When it happens, enjoy it. Savor the strength and renewal it provides.

THIRD TOOL - RECOGNIZE YOUR SACRED NATURE

Sometimes we forget that we are sacred beings. We are sacred, just as the rest of nature is sacred.

I bought two tomato plants one summer, dug a hole for them at the edge of my lawn, surrounded them with fertilizer and healthy soil, and watched them grow. After a couple of months many small tomatoes formed on the plant. Two grew into good sized tomatoes. When I picked them, washed them, and sliced them up, they tasted so sweet and juicy! As I savored their rich flavor, I thanked God for the delicious food. It was a moment of worship, a time when I focused on the lovely taste of tomato and let everything else fade into the background. It created a place in which the tomato and I became one as I marveled at how such a small plant could form such amazing food and what a remarkable accomplishment it was for God to engineer that miracle.

These moments in which we pause to appreciate the beauty of tomato plants, trees, and other elements of nature have profound effects on the world of plants. Our thoughts and emotions, our kindness and affection create a positive reaction in nature that we often don't realize. Recognizing our own sacred nature and how powerful we are can help us understand the importance of directing our thoughts and emotions in ways that encourage and support rather than criticize and tear down. In the big picture, as we give others, including nature, a boost, we are really helping ourselves because we're all connected.

Enjoy the experience of celebrating beauty with appreciation and wonder. In those moments of worship, you become aware of the vast love and the sacred nature you share in harmony with the Oneness that connects us all. Open your heart to this knowing, and feel the strength it provides. No matter where you are, you can find delightful moments of worship.

FOURTH TOOL - LAUGHTER

When the Twinkling Lights/Power Tree let me know it was time to explore the fourth worship tool, suddenly I found myself wanting to laugh. At first I giggled. Then I chortled. My laughter soon turned into rollicking guffaws that made me feel lighter, as though I'd shed several pounds. I felt strong, full of energy, and connected with divine energy all around me. It led to a sense of profound gratitude.

A few minutes later as I strolled down the irrigation ditch bank, I stopped near the Persevering Tree. Once a tall, beautiful cottonwood, all that remains is a stump after someone cut down the tree several years ago. The first time I noticed it, the stump let me know its spirit is alive and well. On this day, I felt the energy of laughter and praise flowing from it as it affirmed for me the worshipful connection that unites us all. Even though all that remained of that once mighty tree was the base of its trunk and the roots that still spread into the ground, the stump carried the gift of laughter and worship. It still found reasons to feel joy.

We praise God with our laughter. No matter what our physical condition, when we laugh, our spirits rise. Our connection with the divine, which flows through all of nature, grows stronger.

FIFTH TOOL - PAY ATTENTION TO DIVINE GUIDANCE

Have you ever felt a nudge to visit or call someone or take some action that didn't make sense to you? If so, you paid attention to divine guidance. It always comes from a place of love and compassion. Your willingness to obey that nudge met a need you hadn't known was there.

We are not the only ones who pay attention to divine guidance. Trees and animals do it too. I suspect they receive inspired nudges from God, and when they follow those nudges, they make a positive difference in someone else's life whether it's a bird, snake, deer or human being. Dogs have been known to smell spikes in a person's blood sugar, soothe reactions to trauma, calm and control kids with autism, and guide people who are blind or challenged in other ways. Some cats in nursing homes know when a resident is about to die and keep them company.

When you feel God nudging you to pay someone a visit, speak a kind word, offer a smile, or touch a tree, don't ignore the divine direction you're receiving. Even trees sometimes need a loving touch, a supportive prayer, an acknowledgement of their value. You never know what a huge difference your small act of kindness or attention could make in someone's life.

SIXTH TOOL - RECOGNIZE YOUR LIMITATIONS

Many people want so much to please others and to be helpful that they find it hard to say no, even when they're asked to do something that makes them feel burdened or overwhelmed. If you find it hard to say no, you understand the feeling of exhaustion and resentment that can come when you agree to do something for which you don't have the time, energy or desire.

Sometimes it's important to say no because someone else can handle the job better, needs the experience, or is better suited for the challenge. When you recognize your limitations, you know when it's the right time to say no. If you can say no and mean it, you will understand that it's wise for you not to tackle what doesn't suit you. Saying no is a way to honor yourself and to recognize the sacred within you. You honor yourself when you handle only those things for which you have the stamina, talent, time and desire.

Though at times you may carry more than your share of the load, if the overall task brings you joy and fulfillment, by all means do what it takes to get the job done. You're playing an important role that gives you pleasure even though you may sometimes grumble about it.

We all go through cycles when certain tasks, organizations, jobs, and careers are fulfilling for us. As time passes, our interests shift, our sense of purpose reorients, circumstances alter, and we know it's time to make a change. We run into trouble when we hang onto our commitment to things we've grown out of. It's time to move on, but we can't let go. Perhaps we find change difficult, we don't want to disappoint others or let them down, we feel guilty about stepping away from an organization that may flounder without our help. But if we stay after we're being guided into new arenas, we become stagnant, our performance suffers. We must recognize our limitations. We can't be all things to all people. We can't continue to grow if we remain chained to what no longer lights our pathway.

Recognize your limitations by realizing that you may not be the right person for the job any more. It's someone else's turn to step into that position because it's time for you to move on, to learn new skills, forge new trails, discover new tasks that bring you joy.

SEVENTH TOOL - BE STILL AND KNOW THAT I AM

One of the most powerful worship tools is stillness. If chaos erupts around you, if nothing seems to go right, if you can't keep your thoughts focused, stop and be still. Tune into the divine presence all around you. Stop trying to think and experience the stillness. Sometimes it only takes a moment for you to recognize a solution to the problem you faced. Other times it takes longer. Take those particles of time wherever you can grab them. Each accumulated second results in greater peace and clarity.

When you're in that place of stillness, it's easier to recognize and value the strengths in yourself and others. If you enjoy the outdoors, notice the gifts that nature offers you. Pick up a pine cone. Discover patterns in it, feel its texture, trace its shape. Examine a leaf, follow its intricate veins, imagine what adventures in flight it has shared with the wind. As you contemplate these things, you will discover stillness. It's in the stillness that you encounter the power, grace and love of divine presence. Relax into it. You will soon feel recharged and ready for whatever lies ahead.

When you focus on the moment, you silence the chatter in your head. It's only when you can let go of the endless things that you still need to do, the anger over some perceived slight, the worry about how you'll pay the rent that you become aware of the divine presence which surrounds you all the time. It's hard to sense heavenly guidance if you can't be still long enough to hear God whisper words of wisdom in your ear – or your heart.

EIGHTH TOOL – PLAYFULNESS

I walked down to the river near my house one day and watched a goose bobbing along in the current. How it got separated from its companions I don't know, but it seemed to enjoy itself. When it saw me, it steered toward the far edge of the river and waddled onto shore, heading toward a clump of cottonwoods. Along the way, it used its beak to explore rocks, weeds and beetles in the sand. Sometimes it made honking sounds as though announcing a discovery. As I watched its playful exploration, I felt at peace.

Another day, I watched my two kittens dash across the room and pounce on each other, their paws batting in play. Then they twisted apart, their backs arched as they eyed each other before making the next lunge. A few moments later, they cuddled on a chair with their eyes closed. They looked peaceful and full of bliss.

When you play, you let go of worries, responsibilities and deadlines. You enjoy the moment spent in joking, running, tumbling, swimming, simply having fun. Allow yourself to curiously explore your circumstances with a hint of playfulness. As your body moves, your muscles relax, and your mind lets go. You will see everything in a different and more pleasant, lighthearted way after you engage in play.

Twice a week I play table tennis with friends who also enjoy the sport. One player said the game helps him concentrate and focus on the moment, so that everything else disappears. That intense awareness allows him to let go of the concerns he carries, the responsibilities he faces. In the moment of play, he finds renewal.

Play is another way to worship. When we worship, we take our concentration off of ourselves and, often without realizing it, we become more aware of God's presence in the joy of the moment. That's when we connect with divinity in a deeper, more intense and delightful way.

Give yourself time to play. It will help you to feel renewed and ready to face whatever comes your way.

NINTH TOOL - ALLOW GOD TO CLEANSE YOU

I spent time with the Fresh Start Tree one day, standing on the irrigation ditch bank and looking at the juniper's branches laden with purple berries. As sometimes happens when I'm near a tree, I felt energy flowing from its roots, moving under the ditch and up into my feet, almost like a huge pipe cleaner traveling through my body. When it reached my throat, it stopped for a while. Something was blocking it, but the energy didn't disperse. Instead, it explored my throat until whatever caused the blockage released, and the energy continued finding its way through my throat, up into my face and out the top of my head. Then it made a big loop up to the top of the Fresh Start tree. From there, it traveled down through its branches, into the ground and back up through my feet. It felt like I'd just gone through an interior car wash, flushing out everything that no longer served me well. When it was over, my energy system flowed more smoothly.

Recently, I needed to contact people who operate my computer's anti-virus program. Somehow, the program had been deleted from my computer. I began an on-line chat with a technician during which I agreed to let him take control of my computer, reinstall the program and make adjustments to help my computer run more quickly and efficiently. I watched the cursor fly across the computer screen. I had no idea what he was doing, but I trusted him to make the appropriate changes. When he was done, my anti-virus program operated again, and my computer performed better.

Just like the technician tuned up my computer, we too need a touch of divine adjustment. It takes an act of trust to allow that clean-up process to take place. If we don't let it happen, life can get more difficult, and we may feel stagnant and unmotivated. The debris that keeps divine energy from freely flowing through us can stop blessings from streaming through us as well.

Are you looking for abundance, happiness, a fulfilling relationship, a new job? It will have a better chance of coming to you if you let God clean out the debris you've been hanging onto. Then loving energy filled with possibilities can flow through you unobstructed.

TENTH TOOL - WHEN LIFE GETS DIFFICULT, PRAY AND PRAISE

When you feel sluggish, when you're barely hanging on or when things fall apart around you, take the time to pray and to praise God. Right in the middle of all that chaos. Express thanks for what is happening right now, no matter how terrible it seems. Be thankful for your circumstances in every moment. Ask for God's help, and express your gratitude that assistance is on its way even if you can't see it yet.

No matter how difficult the circumstances, start praying and sending thoughts of praise to the divine presence that flows through us all. Your circumstances may not change right away, but you are likely to see an improvement in your attitude, a deeper understanding of the bigger picture. That paves the way for other improvements.

Sometimes the circumstances that cause you so much stress, worry, anger, or frustration also help you to grow and expand. As long as you are alive, you expand your understanding, enhance your capabilities, and fine tune your soul. If you experienced a devastating loss, a trying circumstance, or a frightening encounter, you can dwell on what happened. You can wallow in your grief, frustration, or fear, letting it shackle you as you rehash how unfair or disastrous your experience was. It's very human to respond in that way, but you end up stuck in a pit of dejection and turmoil that draws more unpleasantness to you. You were made to grow and expand, to allow yourself to fly higher and freer in spite of challenges. You weren't meant to shrivel into a ball of knotted yarn so hopelessly tangled that you can't function. So choose to see the possibilities, to imagine blessings that can grow out of the problems.

We live among many different people. Connecting with them can give rise to personality clashes, misunderstandings, and disagreements. Those challenges present opportunities. Will you respond to them in a way that pulls you down and chains you to your own negativity, or will you turn to the divine, loving presence that always surrounds you? Will you ask for help and express gratitude for the very circumstances that cause you so much turmoil? The best way to expand and grow in a positive direction is to choose the powerful route of prayer and praise.

Start practicing with simple circumstances. Did your spouse forget to take out the trash, do the laundry, pick up the dry cleaning, fix the meal you wanted, or mow the lawn?

Instead of grumbling, throwing dirty looks, plotting revenge, or calling names, take a deep breath and turn to the divine presence that constantly supports and surrounds you with love. Turn the circumstances over to God and express gratitude for everything that's happened, no matter how ungrateful you feel at the moment. It may take a few moments for you to feel a shift in your attitude, but keep expressing gratitude. Pretty soon you may feel lighter, less weighed down by the circumstances even though the situations may not have changed.

Several times throughout the day snatch a few seconds to express gratitude for everything that's happening in your life, no matter how difficult. If you do that for a couple of weeks, you may see your circumstances change for the better in amazing ways.

Worshipping in an attitude of prayer and praise is powerful. It may feel impossible sometimes. Grit your teeth and try it anyway. As you keep it up, you're likely grit your teeth less and grin more.

CHAPTER 11

CLEANSING TOOLS

Cleansing tools are all about keeping positive energy flowing through you so that you can receive the good things waiting to come into your life.

Among other things, the tools help you stay well grounded. They improve your flexibility so you can move through life more smoothly in spite of circumstances. They help to make you a clearer vessel through which divine love can flow. If you've got a blockage in your energy system, nothing will flow to you or through you as easily as it could if that blockage were dissolved. Cleansing Tools give you ways to keep your energy system in prime condition so that no matter where you are or what you are doing, you can do it better and with greater joy.

FIRST TOOL - STAY WELL GROUNDED

On your journey through this life you have chosen to be on this planet, and it's important for you to stay grounded to Mother Earth. When you're well grounded, you feel more in harmony with your surroundings and you're more content to be here.

Being well grounded lets energy flow through you productively so you're not like a loose wire spraying electricity everywhere. People who work as healers, whether in conventional doctor's offices and hospitals or in alternative settings, cannot be as effective if they aren't well grounded. Without good grounding, they become more susceptible to the negative energies of others. Healing energy that flows from

God, the source of unconditional love, through the healer and into the client must have a way to discharge into the ground or it can make healers feel frazzled, disconnected and clouded by the client's heavy energy that's released during treatment.

Make a practice of feeling your feet as they connect with the surface on which you stand. Sense a flow of energy moving from your feet into the Earth and making a firm connection. Sometimes it helps to imagine a strong rope flowing from deep in the Earth into your feet and up through your body, anchoring you securely to the ground. Some types of shoes make it harder for you to ground effectively. If you have a difficult time grounding when you wear a certain pair of shoes, imagine a way for the energy to flow around your shoes so you can anchor well into the ground in spite of the shoes.

Trees like to help you stay grounded. Their connection to the Earth is so strong that it's easy for them to keep a healthy bond with the planet. The Healing Tree often reminds me to call on it whenever I need help staying grounded, and I am thankful for that assistance. If you feel drawn to that technique, find a tree to which you feel a warm, nurturing relationship. Ask it to help you stay grounded. Ask God to provide the tree with whatever it needs as well.

It may seem silly to think that a tree can help you stay grounded, but German master dowser William de Boer showed that trees and people are connected in profound ways. He used a small dowsing rod to measure the effect that trees have on people. He demonstrated how the energy coming from a large oak could temporarily increase the strength of a human aura, which made the person feel more vital.

When a man who worked with de Boer hugged the oak for two minutes, the man's aura doubled in size. De Boer noted that even when the man and the tree were no longer physically in the same place, the auric field that formed when they touched kept them connected. It is not unusual for people who've made a strong connection with trees to feel the presence of that tree even when they're miles away from it. The tree helps them to stay grounded, to be aware that they are not alone and that they are loved.[23]

Another grounding tool is to imagine a silver thread attached to the top of your head and connected to the sun. Take a little time to feel your connection with the sun. Feel how firm it is, how well it can hold you steady through any circumstance. Sense the strength that connection gives you. Now imagine two golden threads, one lodged on the ball of each foot just below your toes. See each golden thread flowing from the bottoms of your feet deep into the center of the Earth. Allow anything you want to release - any physical or emotional pain, the unpleasant effects of any memory, any false beliefs that no longer serve you well - to flow through your feet and into the ground. Mother Earth is happy to receive those things and to transmute them into something positive. In the process, you not only ground yourself securely to the sky and to the Earth but you let go of whatever is no longer healthy for you.

Whatever grounding technique you decide to use, practice it every day until it becomes second nature. Pretty soon it will be automatic for you to stay grounded. If you become ungrounded, and you will, as soon as you recognize what has happened, you can quickly ground yourself again. Staying grounded will help you in every situation, whether it's at work, at play, at home, or when you're doing energy work for

---

[23] Tompkins, Peter and Bird, Christopher. *The Secret Life of Plants*, Harper, N.Y., 1973, p. 352.

someone. When you're grounded, everything you do becomes a little easier.

SECOND TOOL – LOOK WITHOUT FOCUSING

When you look without focusing, it's easier to see what's real and to let illusions dissolve. You may think you see an object clearly, but it might simply be a mask or a distraction hiding something wonderful that's waiting to be recognized.

The act of looking without focusing can help you see clearly without using past experience, which is often based on false impressions, to determine what something is. When you don't focus on what you're looking at, it's easier not to assume you know what you're seeing. Without the distraction of prejudging what you see, of overthinking it, you can be more casual and relaxed. Then you can more easily let go of worry, anger, guilt, obsession, and a myriad of other details that tend to clutter your mind. They all fall away when you let go of preconceptions and let yourself be in the present moment, where you don't judge what happened in the past or worry about what's going to happen in the future. Then you can more easily see through the foggy window that separates your marred perception of life from the beautiful and magnificent being you really are.

Why is it hard for most of us to understand how beautiful, magnificent and perfect we are? Our own understanding of reality is distorted by false beliefs, misunderstandings, and ways of thinking that no longer serve us well. The veil is so thin between our illusions and what is truly real that, if we gave much thought to it, we might wonder why we can't see through it.

One thing that makes it hard to see what's true is our subconscious mind, which has no filters to sift truth from falsehood. It believes anything we see or hear no matter how untrue or distorted it may be. If someone once told you something hurtful and judgmental such as, "You can't sing well," "You're too fat," "You're not as smart as your brother or sister," your subconscious mind accepted those statements as true no matter how inaccurate they were. We are so surrounded by illusions, misconceptions, and falsehood that it's hard to see the truth unless we learn to look without focusing. Stop seeing what appears to be staring you in the face and, without focusing, look beyond it to discover what's really there.

To practice, look into the distance but don't focus on anything. Everything will look a little blurry. That's okay. Focus on that blurriness, and notice how you're stepping into the present moment where everything else falls away. There are no thoughts of past disappointments or future worries. There's just the splendor of this present moment. Don't try to see images through the blurriness. Just relax even though you don't know what's there. Put your worry button and your need to know button on pause and enjoy the foggy view in this one perfect, peaceful moment.

That's when you start to see what's real. You begin to recognize the immense love that surrounds you, to understand the powerful and capable person you are, and to experience the presence of God in everything. That's when you feel connected to *All that Is*.

It's a time of cleansing, of letting go of all the illusions and misconceptions that have dogged you for so long. Let them slide away. Sense how light you feel when you shed the weight of all the misleading thoughts you've had about yourself. Step into the light and feel clean.

THIRD TOOL - SIT IN NATURE AND LET ITS LOVE CLEANSE YOU

Another way to cleanse yourself is to spend time in nature and feel its love for you.

Connect with nearby trees, bushes, flowers, rivers, brooks, hills or mountains. Feel the presence of the divine, and sense unconditional love pulsing through nature. Allow yourself to absorb that love. Let it wash away everything that makes you feel heavy, negative or stuck. Let it flow through you like a stream of healing water.

If you live near mountains, forests, or the ocean, drive to one of those gorgeous locations. Fill your senses with the beautiful nature that surrounds you. Relax into the knowing that you are cloaked in the presence of God. Feel love flow to you from nature, and soak it in. Let gratitude and love flow out of you to everything and everyone willing to receive it. Breathe in the love that nature offers you. Then breathe out the love you have to offer it. Feel connected to everything. Sense the divine presence of unconditional love sweeping you clean and making you whole.

If you can't get away, if you're confined to a room or if you're harnessed to a tight schedule with little free time, use your imagination. Close your eyes and see yourself in a place that gives you a sense of peace, joy and delight. Feel yourself soak in the unconditional love that surrounds you. Let that love cleanse you of everything that stands in your way of knowing how much you are cherished. Absorb the healing, revitalizing presence of that love, and feel renewed.

When I visited the Portal Tree on the first day of spring, I stood in front of the beautiful juniper and expressed thanks for it. The tree had something to tell me, so I stood quietly, trying to grasp what it had to say. I felt the touch of its presence in my heart, where grief still lingered ten months after the death of my husband. It felt as though the tree were lifting from me a part of that grief. Soon I felt its touch in the muscles along the left side of my body. They began to relax, and my body started to balance. Then the juniper's energy moved to my right side, helping me to relax as I let go of the tension I'd been carrying. I felt more balanced. I stood for a long time in front of that tree, tracking the changes in my body as the juniper helped to clear out some of my grief and stress. Such is the amazing generosity of trees.

FOURTH TOOL - IMMERSE YOURSELF IN THE LIGHT OF UNCONDITIONAL LOVE

This one can be difficult, because it requires that you step away from your ego's desire to be in control. You have trained your ego well to be vigilant and to protect you, but there are times when it must learn to stand aside, to sit obediently quiet. Let go of the need to be right, to win, to have the last word.

After you've told your ego to take some time off, give yourself permission to step into the dimension of unconditional love. There are many ways to do this. Repeat one word such as love, light, beauty, or joy. Say it over and over again until you fall into a mild trance that lets you recognize the presence of divinity in every cell of your body and in every breath that you take. Or imagine yourself being showered by the sparkling presence of love from the top of your head to the bottoms of your feet almost as though you're standing in a waterfall that shimmers with the light of many sunbeams.

Once you feel a hint of that love, even if it's for just a second, take time to let go of old hurts, upsets, disagreements. When you spend time being aware of the unconditional love that surrounds you, everything that once bothered you seems irrelevant and fades away. Soak in that sense of wholeness. Feel cleansed. Know that you are worthy to receive that love no matter what you may have said, done or thought in the past. You are a perfect child of God, unchangeable, whole and so very loved. Let yourself absorb this truth until it permeates every cell of your body, every synapse of your brain, every bone in your skeleton. Know beyond a doubt that you are filled and cleansed with the light of unconditional love.

FIFTH TOOL - RECEIVE GIFTS GIVEN IN LOVE FROM OTHERS

When people offer you gifts in love with no strings attached, they offer you something priceless. It may be as simple as a flower, a book, or a gift card to your favorite restaurant, or it could be something intangible, such as moments of their time when they sense you need a little extra attention. If you can accept their generosity without trying to judge, evaluate, analyze, or dissect it, you will receive a cleansing gift that renews and reinvigorates you. Gifts offered for no other reason than the joy of giving you something lovely are remarkable gestures of love.

Let yourself absorb the purity of that love. If it's hard for you to receive gifts from others because you think they can't afford the gifts or you don't deserve them, remember that you are a holy child of God, who sees you as perfect, worthy to receive gifts given in love. Feel strengthened, cleansed and renewed by the knowledge that someone cared enough to offer you a gift of love from the heart.

Though we chose to spend this lifetime on Earth, the challenges, disappointments, and frustrations we encounter sometimes dull our vision and confuse our discernment. In spite of that, recognize that you, innocent and perfectly whole in God's eyes, are worthy to receive gifts sent to you in love. Even if those gifts are given by someone whose own sense of love is clouded with pain or self-doubt and crusted with the carnage of their wounds, imagine that it comes to you through a shower of cleansing rain which washes away everything that's unhealthy for you. Trust that you can safely receive that gift. Know that when you send gifts in love to others, they will go through that same cleansing shower so that the other person can receive them without any negative attachments.

It's easy to doubt your worthiness to receive such gifts. For just a moment put aside those thoughts of not being good enough or of distrusting others' motives. Bask in the knowing that someone loves you enough to present you with a gift. In spite of how you may have judged yourself, you are worthy to receive this gift, which comes with no strings attached. Open yourself to being loved by other people. Feel yourself accepting their gift. Absorb the strength and nourishment it provides.

SIXTH TOOL - FOCUS ON YOUR BODY'S ENERGY CENTERS

To focus on each of your energy centers, first you have to know where they are. They're sometimes called chakras, a Sanskrit word that means wheel or revolving disc. The chakra system takes higher vibrating energy and converts it to lower vibrating energy that your body can handle without feeling overwhelmed. You have seven major energy centers, and they each have their own functions and purpose. They're associated with acupuncture points in the body that the Chinese have known about and used for thousands of years.

The first center, often called the root chakra, is located at about the place where your legs connect with your torso. It is associated with tribal issues and with our need for food, clothing, shelter and basic life necessities.

The second, also called the belly or navel chakra, is located in the area of your abdomen. It supplies energy for the enjoyment of sexuality and physical attraction in relationships. This chakra helps you to be creative and to find joy in the things you love to do. It affects your appetite and your sense of prosperity and abundance. If you worry about money or carry fear for any reason, you most likely will hold that worry and fear in your second chakra.

The solar plexus, or third chakra, is located slightly above your navel. It relates to your sense of who you are, your self-esteem, personal power and confidence to take action in any situation. Through it you sense your relationship to the universe and to your fellow human beings. It affects your ability to succeed and to take care of yourself.

The fourth, or heart, chakra is related to loving yourself and others unconditionally. It's located near the area of your physical heart. It is capable of holding joy and sorrow, love and fear. As this chakra becomes healthier, it's easier for you to forgive yourself and others. It embodies both your physical and spiritual essence. The healthier your heart chakra is, the more balanced you feel.

The fifth chakra is sometimes called the throat chakra because it's located there. It is an important communication hub among all the chakras. It relates to giving, receiving and speaking the truth. It helps you to express yourself in creative ways. When it's healthy, you find it easy to let others know what you need, how you feel and what you like.

The sixth chakra, sometimes called the brow or third eye chakra, is located about a finger width above your eyebrows in the center of your forehead. It's related to wisdom and intuition. It gives you greater awareness and understanding, clearer insight, and skill in analysis and discernment. It also helps you be more perceptive about the causes for things that happen to you and around you. When your sixth chakra is healthy, your artistic and psychic ability blossoms.

The seventh, or crown, chakra is at the top of your head. When it functions well, it gives you a sense of unity with God. It helps you feel joy and peace. When it's healthy, you bask in the bliss of connection with divine energy that flows through everything. It helps you feel connected to everyone and everything. You understand that there is a reason for everything that occurs even though you may not understand it at the moment.

One way to focus on your energy centers is with the breath. As you think about your root chakra, take a deep breath and let yourself feel the presence of this center. As you breathe in and out, taking slow, deep breaths, acknowledge your first chakra. Express thanks for it and all that it does for you.

Then turn your attention to your second chakra and repeat the process until you have spent time acknowledging, appreciating and thanking God for each of the seven major energy centers in your body. It's one way of giving your body a mini tune-up, like changing the oil and checking the fluid levels in your vehicle. If you have time, say "Thank you," with each breath you take as you move your attention from your crown chakra back down to your root chakra. When you express gratitude, you allow yourself to step into a higher vibrational frequency pattern. In this higher pattern, you are no longer susceptible to the challenges you faced at lower vibrational levels.

For example, if you live at 32 degrees Fahrenheit, you will be plagued by ice. It will be with you all the time. However, if you move to 34 degrees Fahrenheit, which is slightly above where water freezes, you will no longer have to deal with ice. The same is true for vibrational frequency levels. Move to a higher level, and you won't face the problems you faced at a lower level.

As you practice this exercise, you may feel energy moving through your body, cleansing and renewing you. When you make a habit of doing this, it will take you only a few minutes. If you begin each morning this way, you are likely to have a more pleasant, productive day.

SEVENTH TOOL - BE FLEXIBLE SO YOU CAN MOVE

Perhaps, like many people, you feel stuck because you're afraid to rock the boat. You fear change even when you long for it. It might seem easier to stay with the discomfort of what you know than to venture into the possibility of the not yet experienced. New ideas or ways of thinking may threaten to upend your comfortable way of living. They could make your friends or family members feel uncomfortable, threatened or even betrayed if you choose to explore something that they don't consider acceptable. Letting go of the security offered by one job to accept a different opportunity may seem scary and unwise. Even if what you've been doing for years is no longer productive or meaningful, it is familiar. You know what to expect each day, so it makes you feel safe.

There's nothing wrong with keeping your job, staying in a long time relationship, or staying rooted in one place or one belief system. That may be the best place for you, but if you make the decision to stay, make that decision based on a knowing that it's the right thing for you to do. If choosing to stay makes you feel trapped, unfulfilled, or angry, reexamine your motives for staying. If change seems too frightening or impractical, make gentle explorations that provide you with flexibility while staying safely moored to your current situation. Perhaps you can stay in your job, location or relationship while you investigate other ways to grow. Take a class at your local college that appeals to you. Learn a new skill. Join a club that connects you with people who are interested in what you enjoy. Go to a fitness center, take a walk a few times a week, eat healthier foods. Any positive change will promote growth.

Even a small adjustment will help you to be more flexible, and it can lift your spirits. We stagnate if we don't move forward. One thing I do to stay flexible and healthy is to play table tennis twice a week. One of my opponents, who is a better player than I am, reminds me that I have a better chance of returning the ball if I move my feet. And he's right. When I simply extend my arm out farther to reach the ball while keeping my feet stationary, I often lose the point. When I keep my feet moving toward the ball, I not only return it more often but I hit it with enough power that it's harder for my opponent to handle.

Life is like that too. When we're willing to be more flexible, less rooted to one way of thinking or one method of responding to a situation, opportunities are more likely to open for us. At the very least, we discover that we're happier, less judgmental, more willing to experience new things. The more we're willing to be flexible, the more easily we can be led by divine wisdom.

EIGHTH TOOL – LET GO OF WHAT ISN'T HEALTHY FOR YOU

When people think of eliminating unhealthy things from their lives, they sometimes consider changing what they eat or drink. It's important to fuel your body with good nutrients that keep you healthy and that give you better energy. If you're not sure where to begin, your local health food store may have nutrition classes that you can attend to get wise advice about healthy foods for you. Consult a dietician or naturopath, or read some of the many books available on healthy eating habits.

Other people focus on cleaning up the clutter in their house, business, or automobile. Some people have packrat instincts. They find it hard to get rid of anything because they might need it someday. Those instincts can become so pronounced that hoarders fill their homes, storage rooms or cars so full of old newspapers, magazines, gadgets, furniture or tools that they can hardly find a pathway through the clutter. Excessive clutter saps energy. It creates a heavy atmosphere that makes it harder for people to think clearly and to enjoy their lives.

When your life becomes compromised by too much junk, it's time to start letting go of things you no longer need. That can be hard if you have emotional attachments to them. Ask yourself questions such as these. Can you easily find what you need? Do you enjoy living with so much clutter? Do you feel embarrassed about having people come to your house because of how messy it looks? Have the courage to give yourself an honest answer.

If you're tired of the clutter and want to clean it up, you may be stymied because the project seems so massive. Don't try to clean up the entire house. Instead, choose one room and clean it up. Don't move stuff from one room to another. Instead, put what you're willing to part with into plastic bags and donate them to a thrift store or service organization. Knowing that your items will go to someone who needs them may help you let them go with greater ease.

Let's face it. The job won't be easy, but as you clean up one room and see how nice it looks, you may be more motivated to tackle another room, then another. If you can't handle the task by yourself, find a friend, counselor, or psychotherapist who can help you discover what's keeping you tied to the clutter and what you can do to sever those ties.

As hard as it can be to change eating habits and declutter a house, it can be even harder to change your attitude. What thoughts and emotions do you fill your mind and heart with? Are they healthy, or do you carry a grudge or hold resentments? Are you constantly rehashing old wounds? If you can't or won't forgive someone for a real or perceived injustice, if you hang onto hurt feelings, you are carrying emotional clutter that's making you as stuck as though you had stepped in quicksand. You can gripe, curse, and accuse others, but with every complaint you'll sink deeper into the quicksand of your own anger. That sinks you into a lower vibrational frequency where more negative challenges await you.

The only way to cleanse yourself of the emotional junk that keeps you stuck is to forgive. That doesn't mean letting people off the hook or letting them back into your life. If they committed a crime, they must appear before a judge and serve their sentence. If they abused you or mistreated you in some other way, you don't have to see them ever again. Even if you never associate with them in the future, you must let go of the emotional ties that connect you. Should you decide to hold onto your anger, feelings of injustice, or desire for revenge, you will find yourself locked in a prison cell of your own making. That cell locks you into the negative feelings that separate you from the peace and happiness you seek.

Someone may not have committed a crime against you, but they've hurt your feelings or said something that upset you. If you frequently rehash those hurts in your mind, you're chained to the past. You'll remain stuck as long as you hang onto those grudges, resentments and hurt feelings.

Letting go of past hurts takes time. Sometimes it's so hard that you may need to seek professional help from a psychotherapist or other mental health practitioner. Perhaps you don't want to let go of that pain because it serves you in some way. It might make you feel safer, or it could give you someone to blame when you can't find the success you seek. It could mask a feeling of guilt you've buried deep within yourself that's too painful to face.

Talking with a friend might help you take the first steps toward letting go of the emotional junk that keeps you from moving forward. You may be able to find a group of people who have faced painful life situations such as losing a child, being the victim of a crime, or facing the aftermath of divorce. Hospitals, churches, schools or other organizations often sponsor such groups, and you can participate free of charge or for a small fee. Knowing you're not the only one facing your issue goes a long way toward helping you work through it.

Often, the negative feelings you harbor aren't your own. You've picked them up from someone else without realizing it. To let go of those feelings that don't belong to you, use the cord cutting exercise. With your hands, slice through the space in front of you as though you were using a knife to cut a loaf of bread. As you make that motion, say, "I cut the cords between me and (name of the person) with love, forgiveness and compassion." Ask Archangel Michael to help you cut those cords. When those unwanted thoughts crop up, cut the cords again.

If the negative thoughts do originate with you, the cord cutting exercise is still effective. Any time negative or resentful thoughts arise about a person or situation, cut the cords that are binding you to that person or thing. Keep cutting the cords as long as necessary. If you don't cut those cords, they will continue to bind you to negative attitudes. The people with whom you're upset won't be bound by those cords unless they choose to be. They're not the ones carrying the grudge. But those cords will bind you and keep you stuck in the rut of your own negative emotions until you can let them go.

Forgiving others isn't about absolving them of guilt or responsibility. It's about freeing yourself from the weight of your own heavy emotions that bog you down so you can't move. When you're stuck, you can't fulfill the purpose for which you came into this life. Once you let go of those heavy burdens, you will feel lighter and more clear headed. You'll start to enjoy your life once again.

NINTH TOOL - LET OTHERS LOVE YOU

This tool is similar to the fifth tool, "Receive Gifts Given in Love from Others." It differs slightly from it because the tool of "Let Others Love You" refers to accepting their love. The fifth tool, on the other hand, involves receiving gifts that are given to you in love. Receiving a gift involves agreeing to take it, while accepting a gift shows your willingness to put it to good use. We are surrounded by more love than we can imagine. The many divine helpers who have been assigned to assist us want to lavish us with their love, but if we only receive it without applying the gift in some way to our lives, we can't experience how healing and cleansing the love that comes with that gift can be.

It's easy to be so burdened by our worries and responsibilities that we forget to notice how much love blankets us. It comes not only from people but from nature, angels and other spirit helpers assigned to us. They are doing their best to reveal that love to us.

Too often we wall ourselves off from love because we don't want to be hurt or betrayed, we don't think we're worthy of receiving love, or we can't imagine why someone would want to love us. Love is the most powerful, healing emotion in this universe, more powerful than anything else, and it's ours if we choose to accept it. It is life changing and nurturing, and it will fill our lives with more joy than we could imagine.

But first we have to overcome our fear of accepting it. We have to let go of whatever else we're clutching, whether it's grief, fear, righteous indignation, or something else, so we can reach out to welcome the love that's waiting for us. Perhaps we want someone to give us something, and if they don't or can't, we feel let down, cheated, betrayed, unloved. Letting others love us does not mean that we allow them to provide for us, to give us what we think we want or need. That kind of attitude does not describe love. Instead, it describes a sense of entitlement or a desire to manipulate the other person into giving us what we want.

When we let others love us, we let them send us the energy of love. It is uplifting and strengthening, and it accepts us without judgment and with no strings attached. Surrounded by such incredible love, we begin to see ourselves as the perfect, loving, unchanging and powerful beings that God knows we are. If you accept love from others, you are accepting their recognition of the awesome being you truly are.

TENTH TOOL - LET THE WIND OF GOD CLEANSE YOU

When wind gusts through an area, it stirs up trash, blows lost school papers onto fences, and knocks dead or dying branches from bushes and trees. We have whirlwinds in northwest New Mexico, where I live. They have been known to whoosh pickup camper shells from their stowed positions and dash them to bits in the middle of a highway or hillside. People who weren't at home to see the whirlwind think someone robbed them or vandalized their camper shell, but it was just the wind.

The wind of God is powerful too. Though it's not really wind, when you let it sweep through you, it cleans out the junk and trash with which you sometimes clutter your mind and heart. It's a gentle but effective power. You can invite that healing wind to cleanse you when you spend time in quietness, whether in prayer, in meditation, or in some activity that calms you. Ask God to cleanse you of impurities, illusions, misconceptions that no longer serve you well. Those beliefs may once have helped you, but now you're in a place where they'll hold you back if you can't let them go.

Many of you give your house a good spring cleaning. You sweep, mop, dust, and donate items that you no longer need. Afterwards, your house sparkles, looks neater and roomier and even feels lighter. When you let the wind of God cleanse you, you feel brighter and lighter too.

Why not treat yourself to a God-force cleaning job at least once a year? You'll be surprised how many more opportunities and delightful surprises flow your way when you have room to receive them. What no longer serves you has been swept away, providing more space.

CHAPTER 12

THE CONNECTION CONTINUES

Over the years, trees have continued to communicate with me and I with them in ways that help us both. I am increasingly aware that trees are one avenue to my own deeper wisdom, my Higher Self that remains a constant, dependable guide. My connection to trees is a frequent reminder that we are all One, all connected to God, to that divine source that created us and loves us unconditionally.

The Power Tree has made it a point to go to places and events where I gave away my power. It collects it and brings it back to me. All I have to do is accept it. And, of course, I have. The incredible kindness of the Power Tree touches me deeply. More recently I've become aware of its trunk standing around me. Whenever I do something that gives my power away, the trunk blocks the power from leaving and sends it right back to me. Because of that, I'm more able to recognize what those negative situations are that trigger my decision to deplete my power.

Many of the trees have come to me at different times, helping me when I needed extra strength and stamina. They each have their own energy, and that energy often has different colors. The Power Tree's is white, while the Healing Tree's is blue, and the Wings Tree's is green. When I am in need, they each send their energy to me. It swirls through my system in varied colors.

The last time I returned from Alaska, I took time to visit the Healing Tree so it could download whatever message Alaska trees had sent to my trees. As usual, I had no idea if I carried a message or what that message might be. When I stood by the Healing Tree, being grateful for all it has meant to me over the years, I felt something I'd never felt before. It was as if the tree were using a cloud comb to gently sweep through my aura and find the message. I asked if the tree would share the message with me. Into my mind came the words, "Stand tall. I recognize your worth." Now, wherever I go if a tree catches my attention, I tell it, "Stand tall. I recognize your worth." And I stand a little taller too, because that message is for me, and for all of us, as well. We can all stand a little taller because the divine presence in each of us recognizes our worth.

All the trees continue to like receiving Reiki and prayer. They reach out to me when they need help, and they support me when I need a boost. Trees have much to offer anyone who is willing to approach them with respect and appreciation.

They respond well to love and gratitude. They like to be acknowledged for what they do for us on both a physical and spiritual level. When you take a few minutes to spend time with trees and do it with respect and love, those few minutes can reap abundant emotional and spiritual rewards for you. Take a chance, even if you feel foolish communicating with a tree, and find out if it works for you. You'll lose only a few moments of your time, and you may discover amazing benefits.

About Margaret Cheasebro

A freelance writer who has won many state and national awards for her magazine articles, Margaret Cheasebro is also a Reiki Master and shaman. Her young adult fantasy/reality novel, *The Healing Tree,* is available from Casa de Snapdragon LLC. Her ebook, *Healing and Growing with Reiki: Exploring Reiki I, II and III (Reiki Master)* may be purchased as a Kindle book on Amazon.

She has written teacher activity guides for several chapter books, among them *Belle's Star, Belle's Trial,* and *Belle's Challenge,* books written by Connie Gotsch and told from a dog's point of view.

A retired elementary school counselor, she continues to write books and to pen articles for regional magazines. She is a frequent contributor to Majestic Living Magazine. She enjoys playing table tennis with other ping pong enthusiasts in Farmington, NM. For information on attending a workshop about connecting with trees, you may contact her at *mwriter4571@yahoo.com.*

Recent Releases From

Casa de Snapdragon

The Healing Tree
Margaret Cheasebro
ISBN: 978-1-937240-60-8
Genre: Young Adult (YA)

When three children meet at summer camp, they discover that in a past life they fled from an evil woman who tried to steal their blood and their powerful connection to nature so she could rule the world. To their horror, the children find the evil woman at camp, posing as Jasmine, the rich owner's girlfriend, and she still wants their blood. A magical cottonwood helps them flee to a Pueblo village that stood on the camp site 900 years ago. Using the time traveling cottonwood, Jasmine joins forces with Sage Handler. Mysterious Baba, the summer camp's caretaker, lends his aid as the kids and star warriors, who befriend them, try to thwart Jasmine's plans. Can the children believe in themselves, outwit their enemies, and defeat Jasmine before she achieves her goal of ruling the world?

Grabbing the Apple: An Anthology of New York Women Poets
Edited by Terri Muuss and M.J. Tenerelli
ISBN: 978-1-937240-70-7
Genre: Poetry, Women Poets

The story of Eve has been, more often than not, interpreted by men. Eve has been presented as impulsive, disobedient and ignorant. But what if Eve were the real hero and mother of us all? Where would we be had she never looked for knowledge, asked the important questions, challenged the powers that be? The women whose work has been anthologized in this collection are as bold as New York, as brave as Eve.

A Witches' Garden
Trish Breedlove
ISBN: 978-1-937240-68-4
Genre: Gardening

From the very basics of where to place your garden, how big should it be, what plants should you include all the way down to how to use the bounty of your harvest, Trish leaves no stone unturned and the only questions that remain are; When will you start your own and What are you waiting for?

Geographic: A Novel of Time and Space
Miriam Sagan
ISBN: 978-1-937240-62-2
Genre: Biographies & Autobiographies

Miriam Sagan has written a book that tells in poetic beauty the often difficult and frequently uplifting history of her own life and challenges as she tumbles through the mixture of events that helped contribute to the writer that she is today.

Made in the USA
Las Vegas, NV
01 October 2022